Teaching Excellence II:

A RESEARCH-BASED WORKBOOK *for* TEACHERS

ism Publications

Teaching Excellence II:
A Research-Based Workbook for Teachers

By M. Walker Buckalew, Ph.D., ISM Executive Consultant, with
Barbara J. Beachley, Ed.M., ISM Associate Consultant

Independent School Management, Inc.
1316 N. Union Street, Wilmington, DE 19806

Telephone: 302-656-4944 · FAX: 302-656-0647

isminc.com
pubs@isminc.com

Disclaimer: Independent School Management, Inc., (ISM) provides management consulting and other services to private-independent schools. ISM is not a law firm. No service or information provided by ISM in any verbal or written form (including this book) should be construed as legal advice. ISM specifically advises schools to consult with legal counsel qualified in their jurisdiction regarding all legal matters (including the hiring, rewarding, and terminating of personnel). All Web links and references in this book are correct as of the publication date, but may have become inactive or otherwise modified since that time.

ISM Consortium Member: $24.00 · Nonmember: $30.00

Paperback ISBN-13: 978-1-883627-13-3
Paperback ISBN-10: 1883627133

Contents

History and Overview

Independent School Management (ISM) has provided advice and counsel to private-independent schools since the mid-1970s. A data-driven organization, ISM launches research projects regularly in pursuit of various hypotheses.

This book is the result of two research projects spanning more than two decades (and more than 15 years of pertinent experience between the two). One of them was the seminal project in its examination of factors influencing student performance, student satisfaction, and student enthusiasm. The other was a partial replication and statistical strengthening of the original project. This book treats the findings of both.

The ISM International Model Schools Project ran for six years, from 1989 to 1995, and entailed ISM on-site data collection expeditions—usually three per year—to eight to nine private-independent schools annually. The project focused upon relevant factors in student performance, satisfaction, and enthusiasm and, secondarily, on teacher performance, satisfaction, and enthusiasm.

That project's outcomes produced two books, numerous articles for ISM's periodicals, and ISM's Meaningful Faculty Evaluation system. Those building blocks served, in turn, as the foundation for later ISM studies of School Head leadership and Board President leadership. Finally, the original outcomes and subsequent research projects were layered systematically into the several iterations of the ISM Stability Markers and, more recently, the 20 ISM Success Predictors for the 21st Century.

In the school year 2010–11, ISM conducted a one-year partial replication of the original project, this time with strengthened statistical treatments, with eight private-independent schools. The mix of schools, as with the original project, included the full range of possible grade configurations, religiously affiliated and secular, single-sex and coed, and boarding and day.

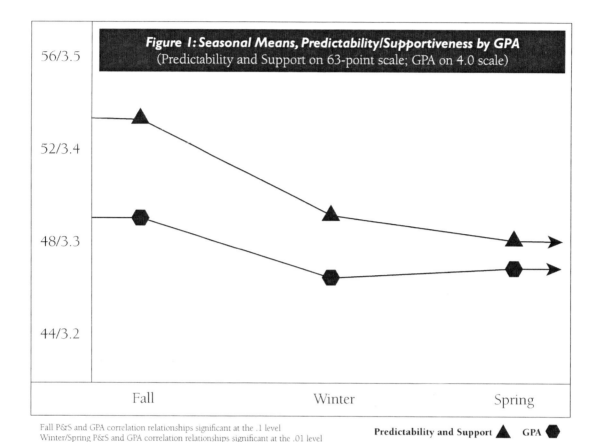

Figure 1: Seasonal Means, Predictability/Supportiveness by GPA
(Predictability and Support on 63-point scale; GPA on 4.0 scale)

Fall P&S and GPA correlation relationships significant at the .1 level
Winter/Spring P&S and GPA correlation relationships significant at the .01 level

Predictability and Support ▲ GPA ⬢

In ISM's research, a statistical correlation has been firmly established between teacher-determined classroom conditions called by ISM "predictability and supportiveness" (as perceived through the eyes of students) and student performance, student-perceived satisfaction, and student-perceived enthusiasm. These classroom conditions are not a function of pedagogical "style," teacher "personality," or age of student. These conditions can be created by the application (by teachers) of a cluster of characteristics and principles.

This volume presents these characteristics and principles in workbook form.

"Predictability and supportiveness"—the paired set of critical classroom conditions and organizational ingredients—have been found in these studies in greatest strength in school environments in which students perceive that:

– the rule/reward structure is strong, but also intelligible and fair from the student perspective;

– faculty/administration/coaching responses are consistent, fair, and accurate from the student perspective, in regard to what is positively or negatively reinforced (both academically and behaviorally); and

– the faculty, administration, and coaching staffs appear to the students genuinely to desire student success and work to elicit that success, but nonetheless provide accurate—not inflated—reinforcement (as implied by the first two items in this list).

(The measuring device for these characteristics, the Student Experience Profile II, may be seen in Appendix B of this book. This instrument is designed for use by students in grades 5–12.)

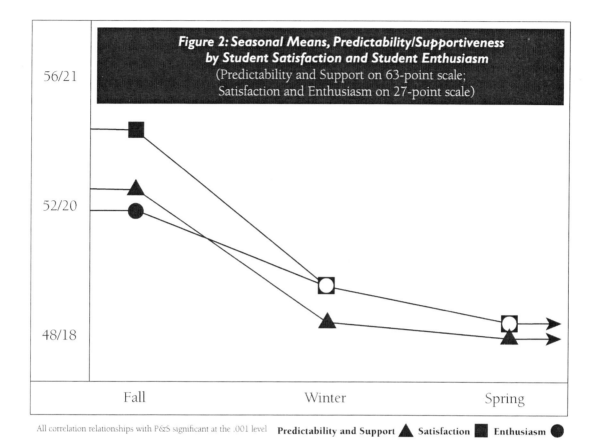

Figure 2: Seasonal Means, Predictability/Supportiveness by Student Satisfaction and Student Enthusiasm
(Predictability and Support on 63-point scale; Satisfaction and Enthusiasm on 27-point scale)

All correlation relationships with P&S significant at the .001 level   **Predictability and Support** ▲ **Satisfaction** ■ **Enthusiasm** ●

A rapid-look summary of the research relationships is presented in Figures 1 and 2. In Figure 1, predictability and supportiveness levels (P&S) are shown as they were found in ISM's most recent study for fall, winter, and spring grading periods. Shown in the same figure (with a different scale along the vertical axis) are the cumulative grade-point averages (GPA) of students in the study. GPAs, as expected (based on earlier ISM findings), were highest in fall, lowest in winter, and intermediate in spring. Measures of P&S, on the other hand, were highest in fall, dropped considerably in winter, and declined further in spring.

The correlation statistic showed a significant relationship between P&S and GPA in the fall, but at the lowest traditionally acceptable level of social-science "significance" (.1). The correlation strengthened throughout the year, reaching significance levels of .01 in both winter and spring. This is suggested graphically in Figure 1 by the decreasing gap between P&S measures and GPAs as the school year progresses.

See Table I in Appendix E for actual correlations and means, and for a fuller discussion of the most recent research project.

In Figure 2, predictability and supportiveness levels (P&S) are, as in Figure 1, shown as they were found in ISM's most recent study for fall, winter, and spring grading periods. Shown in the same figure (with a different scale along the vertical axis) are student-perceived satisfaction (SAT) and student-perceived enthusiasm (ENTH) levels for each season. Measures for all six of these variables declined throughout the school year.

The correlation statistic showed a highly significant relationship between P&S and SAT and between P&S and ENTH in each season of the school year. The strength of this relationship (.001), already powerful in the fall, continued to strengthen in both winter and spring grading periods. This is suggested graphically in Figure 2 by the decreasing gap between measures for P&S and SAT and between measures for P&S and ENTH as the school year progresses.

See Table 1 in Appendix E for actual correlations and means, and for a fuller discussion of the most recent research project.

Predictability and Supportiveness: The ISM School Culture Matrix

A school culture strongly marked by "predictability" and "supportiveness" ("High P/High S") in the environment can be expected to display specific organizational characteristics. This can be said, as well, regarding the other three possible culture-pairings: high predictability and low supportiveness ("High P/Low S"); low predictability and high supportiveness ("Low P/High S"); and low predictability and low supportiveness ("Low P/Low S").

A discussion of these four quadrants and a graphic display follows.

High Predictability/High Supportiveness (High P/High S)

- Predictability and supportiveness sustained over time
- Healthy student and faculty cultures
- Balanced leadership (both prescriptive and nonprescriptive)
- Consistent and constructive evaluation

In the "High P/High S" quadrant, each of these four items implies the other three, i.e., it is difficult to implement one of these extremely well without simultaneously doing extremely well with the others. In regard to faculty evaluation, for example, "balanced leadership" that is "both prescriptive and nonprescriptive" would often mean the administration chooses to dictate the structure, ground rules, and research base for the faculty evaluation system (thus, "prescriptive"). At the same time, the administration may choose to delegate the creation of the evaluation system's specific criteria for excellence to a faculty task unit, subject to the administration's final approval ("nonprescriptive").

Outcomes of such an approach are likely to include (a) more consistent and constructive evaluation; (b) a healthier faculty culture; and (c) a more predictable and supportive environment, as seen through the eyes of the teachers themselves. This is but one among countless possible examples of the effects of leaders' "balanced"—prescriptive and nonprescriptive—decisions on organizational process, culture, and performance.

High Predictability/Low Supportiveness (High P/Low S)

- Bureaucratic evaluation
- Rules, not reasons
- Authoritarian leadership
- Culture of fear and resentment
- Conformist environment

Figure 3: The ISM School Culture Matrix

PREDICTABILITY QUAD	OPTIMAL PERFORMANCE QUAD
High P/Low S • Bureaucratic evaluation • Rules, not reasons • Authoritarian leadership • Culture of fear and resentment • Conformist culture	**High P/High S** • Predictability and support sustained over time • Healthy student and faculty cultures • Balanced leadership (prescriptive and nonprescriptive) • Consistent/constructive evaluation
Low P/Low S • Gossip-ridden environment • Culture of fear and uncertainty • Leadership failure • Ineffective evaluation • Adult-centered culture • Fragmented faculty culture	**Low P/High S** • Culture of uncertainty • Supervision for praise, not purpose • Consensus-based leadership • Conflict-averse leadership and culture
TOXIC QUAD	**SUPPORTIVENESS QUAD**

High Predictability

Low Predictability

Low Supportiveness ←————————————→ High Supportiveness

Note: The ISM School Culture Matrix, "Instrument, Scoring Instructions, and Scoring Chart," can be found in Appendix A. Readers who are interested in the research minutiae may wish to read Appendix E, "The Replication Project: Detail."

The list above represents the (expected) major characteristics of an organization that is strong in predictability but weak in supportiveness. Such a school is weak in creating an environment in which *the followers*—teachers, in their relationship to administrators; and students, in their relationship to teachers/coaches/administrators—*are confident that their leaders wish them success* (whether they are as yet successful or not). While "High P/Low S" organizations tend to develop all five of the characteristics shown above, there may be exceptions.

For example, an authoritarian administrator who is perceived not as "mean," but as goal-focused to the exclusion of all else, will perhaps be able to steer clear of the worst aspects of a "culture of fear and resentment" (just as an authoritarian teacher may not consistently produce fear or resentment in students). But, without leadership attentiveness to the "supportiveness" component (producing a settled confidence on the part of the followers that the leader truly wishes their success), fear and resentment will always be a heartbeat away.

Successful military combat units are "High P/Low S" with good reason, i.e., errors can result in death to the troops themselves and, beyond that, to those whom they endeavor to protect. In contrast, in teaching/learning organizations such as schools, experimentation (such as "action research" for teachers and electronic trial-and-correction software for students) has a necessary function. It is *freedom-within-structure* that tends to foster high levels of performance, satisfaction, and enthusiasm at both the teacher and student levels. Predictability is essential, but without supportiveness, predictability is ultimately self-defeating in school contexts.

Low Predictability/High Supportiveness (Low P/High S)

- Culture of uncertainty

- Supervision for praise, not purpose

- Consensus-based leadership

- Conflict-averse leadership and culture

This is the "natural" quadrant toward which educators—both teachers and administrators—tend to gravitate. This is the case because educators are usually most comfortable in environments characterized by intellectual give-and-take within an academic society of equals. Ideas predominate; the most worthy ideas prevail.

Effective PK–12 schools for children and adolescents, however, are not graduate seminars. Schools have missions, purposes, and outcomes, coupled with paying "customers." The latter commit significant portions of their families' resources to private-independent schools in order that their children may experience those missions, purposes, and outcomes.

And this implies hierarchy. Those at or near the top of those hierarchies determine the school mission, purposes, and desired outcomes. Thus, "predictability" is established by means of organizational structures that make the mission-specific "deliverables" likely to materialize.

When this "predictability" component is given little or no meaningful attention, "supportiveness"—teachers' confidence that the administrators desire their success and students' confidence that their teachers desire their success—may reach high levels. However, without "predictability," it is likely that uncertainty, "false-positive" reinforcement, and a "franchise mentality" among teachers will eventually come to predominate. High (mission-specific) performance, high (mission-related) satisfaction, and high (mission-related) enthusiasm are the first casualties of the "Low P/High S" environment.

Low Predictability/Low Supportiveness (Low P/Low S)

- Gossip-ridden environment
- Culture of fear and uncertainty
- Leadership failure
- Ineffective evaluation
- Adult-centered culture
- Fragmented faculty culture

Where both "predictability" and "supportiveness" are in short supply, toxic environments develop, even though there may be numerous individuals who manage to avoid the toxicity. The reverse of the familiar adage, "a rising tide lifts all boats," comes inexorably into play. The prevailing "low tide" will frustrate these (often heroic) individual efforts to provide high levels of performance, satisfaction, and enthusiasm for the students.

Seldom can such toxicity be corrected without, in James Collins's memorable metaphor, "getting the wrong people off the bus and the right people on the bus and in the right seats." This does not mean that teachers should not challenge ideas or contribute their own thoughts and expertise to school discussions, which is part of a healthy school culture. It means, rather, that teachers must do this with student performance, student satisfaction, and student enthusiasm at the heart of their motivation.

Notes:

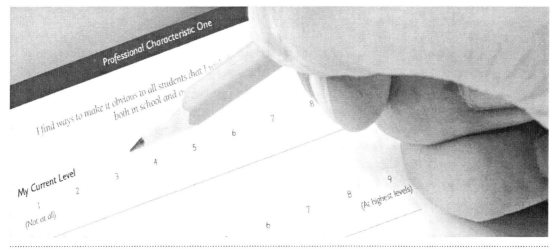

Self-Directed Analysis (Part One)

There is no single "correct" way to use the material in this workbook. From this point on, the rest of this material will deal with developing the teacher-student, teacher-teacher, and teacher-administrator implications of ISM's "predictability and supportiveness" findings as they apply to your school. Here are a few of your choices.

- Work through the rest of the material as an individual. Use the workbook-like pages to score yourself, to reach decisions about changes in your own approach that you might wish to attempt, and to set professional development goals for yourself.

- Do the same in cooperation with one or more of your peers. Meet periodically to discuss these ideas, to initiate individual or small-group (pedagogical) trials (a form of "action research"), and to compare notes week-by-week and month-by-month.

- Involve your administrator(s) to:

    (a) perform a whole-faculty self-scoring on the "ISM School Culture Matrix Instrument and Scoring Chart" (Appendix A);

    (b) discuss the outcomes vis-à-vis the ISM School Culture Matrix (shown in the previous chapter);

    (c) administer the Student Experience Profile II (Appendix B);

    (d) administer the Faculty Culture Profile II (Appendix C);

(e) incorporate the Characteristics of Professional Excellence II (Chapters 2–3, pp. 103–110) into your approach to faculty evaluation; and/or

(f) in other creative ways, integrate your own work in this book with the in-parallel work of your colleagues. Do this with the long-term goal of establishing and maintaining your faculty culture's position in the upper-right quadrant of the ISM School Culture Matrix.

The material following in this chapter is designed to address the question of how your current approach to teaching "plays" in the context of ISM's findings regarding the student experience. What follows in this chapter is a presentation of the 13 "Characteristics of Professional Excellence" found in ISM's Student Experience Study to have a statistical relationship to student performance, student satisfaction, and student enthusiasm. (Chapter Three will present a second tier of 22 related characteristics.)

Use the pages following as your workbook. Respond to the rating scales that are provided, make notes in the margins, converse about the items with your peers.

Four rating scales are provided for each of the 13 characteristics. You may choose to respond only to the first scale in each case (the one referring to your current approach). The other scales will allow you to record your aspirations, your entire faculty's "averaged" ratings (in your own estimation), and your entire faculty's *range* of approaches (again, of course, in your own estimation).

The scale is one through nine; nine is "high" on each item.

Note: Appendix F (pp. 103–110) shows these same "Characteristics of Professional Excellence" in a format designed for use as a component in your faculty evaluation system, thereby connecting your faculty evaluation approach to student performance, satisfaction, and enthusiasm. When used in that context, you would rate yourself on each item, compare your self-ratings with your faculty supervisor's ratings of you, and use that (annual) conversation as a basis for continuing along your career-long professional development pathway.

Professional Characteristic One

I find ways to make it obvious to all students that I wish them success every day, both in school and outside of school.

My Current Level

1	2	3	4	5	6	7	8	9

(Not at all)   (At highest levels)

My Three-Year Goal

1	2	3	4	5	6	7	8	9

(Not at all)   (At highest levels)

My Estimate of Our Faculty Average

1	2	3	4	5	6	7	8	9

(Not at all)   (At highest levels)

My Estimate of Our Faculty Range (use brackets)

1	2	3	4	5	6	7	8	9

(Not at all)   (At highest levels)

Comment: This is a statement *not* about your personal/professional demeanor, e.g., warm, welcoming, upbeat, or cold, standoffish, downbeat. It is a statement about your pedagogical technique: that is, about the act of setting high expectations and making them clear (see Characteristics No. 3 and 4, following) **and** of communicating by words and actions your determination to assist the students in reaching those expectations.

Professional Characteristic Two

I find ways to make it obvious to all students that I want them to become better, more virtuous people (in ways consistent with our school's stated purposes and projected outcomes for our graduates).

My Current Level

| 1 | 2 | 3 | 4 | 5 | 6 | 7 | 8 | 9 |

(Not at all)   (At highest levels)

My Three-Year Goal

| 1 | 2 | 3 | 4 | 5 | 6 | 7 | 8 | 9 |

(Not at all)   (At highest levels)

My Estimate of Our Faculty Average

| 1 | 2 | 3 | 4 | 5 | 6 | 7 | 8 | 9 |

(Not at all)   (At highest levels)

My Estimate of Our Faculty Range (use brackets)

| 1 | 2 | 3 | 4 | 5 | 6 | 7 | 8 | 9 |

(Not at all)   (At highest levels)

Comment: This is a statement *not* about your commitment to the school mission—which is assumed—but about your willingness and ability to make this commitment overt. Since mission statements implicitly or explicitly assert the school's intention to develop good people and good citizens, your "public" references to, and insistence upon, virtuous conduct (e.g., conduct that exemplifies truth, honesty, integrity, fair play) comprise core characteristics of professional excellence.

Professional Characteristic Three

I set clearly articulated standards for student academic performance.

My Current Level

1	2	3	4	5	6	7	8	9
(Not at all)								*(At highest levels)*

My Three-Year Goal

1	2	3	4	5	6	7	8	9
(Not at all)								*(At highest levels)*

My Estimate of Our Faculty Average

1	2	3	4	5	6	7	8	9
(Not at all)								*(At highest levels)*

My Estimate of Our Faculty Range (use brackets)

1	2	3	4	5	6	7	8	9
(Not at all)								*(At highest levels)*

Comment: This is a statement *not* about your own scoring and grading system itself, but about your ability and willingness to illuminate the nature of your academic expectations, i.e., *not* about explaining that 90–93 = A- and 94–97 = A and 98–100 = A+, but delineating (in age-appropriate fashion, of course) the subject-specific levels of mastery that you expect from your students. An illustration of this might entail providing students with examples (in advance of an assignment) of submissions that you would grade as A, B, C, and so on, or involving your students in the development of the rubric.

Professional Characteristic Four

I set reasonable, defensible standards for student behavior.

My Current Level

I	2	3	4	5	6	7	8	9

(Not at all)   (At highest levels)

My Three-Year Goal

I	2	3	4	5	6	7	8	9

(Not at all)   (At highest levels)

My Estimate of Our Faculty Average

I	2	3	4	5	6	7	8	9

(Not at all)   (At highest levels)

My Estimate of Our Faculty Range (use brackets)

I	2	3	4	5	6	7	8	9

(Not at all)   (At highest levels)

Comment: This is a statement *not* about schoolwide rules and regulations, but about the behavioral expectations you develop for students in your own classroom. The statement implies that your behavioral expectations should be spelled out—possibly in writing and posted in your classroom—and, beyond that, should be explained in ways that are intelligible to your students. (It is worth remembering that "bad laws make hard cases." Your standards for student behavior in your classroom should relate to the school mission and should be viewed by students as *reasonable* applications of that mission.) As a community-building opportunity at the beginning of the year, consider involving your students in the development of classroom rules, etiquette, and expectations.

Professional Characteristic Five

*I am continually alert to displays of unkindness among students
in my efforts to ensure a safe physical and emotional environment.*

My Current Level

1	2	3	4	5	6	7	8	9
(Near zero)								(At highest levels)

My Three-Year Goal

1	2	3	4	5	6	7	8	9
(Near zero)								(At highest levels)

My Estimate of Our Faculty Average

1	2	3	4	5	6	7	8	9
(Near zero)								(At highest levels)

My Estimate of Our Faculty Range (use brackets)

1	2	3	4	5	6	7	8	9
(Near zero)								(At highest levels)

Comment: This statement references your alertness to a widespread and pervasive threat to the fabric of any healthy student culture. "Mean" students—who may, in fact, be "mean" in no other ways—may tend to "pick on" other students in subtle ways even *during* teacher-centered class sessions, and in not-so-subtle ways during small-group work, in hallways, in bathrooms, before or after school, and/or at other times when the focus of your attention is not specifically on them. You cannot eradicate unkind behavior, but you can both heighten your sensitivity to this culture-destroying phenomenon and, working with your colleagues, develop more effective methods—both classroom-specific and schoolwide—of combating it.

Professional Characteristic Six

In confrontations with students, I conduct myself in ways that leave students' dignity intact regardless of the nature of the issue or infraction.

My Current Level

1	2	3	4	5	6	7	8	9
(Never)								(Always)

My Three-Year Goal

1	2	3	4	5	6	7	8	9
(Never)								(Always)

My Estimate of Our Faculty Average

1	2	3	4	5	6	7	8	9
(Never)								(Always)

My Estimate of Our Faculty Range (use brackets)

1	2	3	4	5	6	7	8	9
(Never)								(Always)

Comment: Confrontations with certain students may be inevitable. This statement underscores the importance of developing the skill-set to conduct a confrontation without in any way demeaning the student(s) being confronted. For most teachers, implementing this Professional Characteristic successfully implies (a) a steady focus during the confrontation on the unacceptable *actions* of the student, rather than on the student's personality or character; and (b) learning to create opportunities for inclusion that can be delivered as soon after the confrontation as realistically possible, e.g., "Is that absolutely clear, then? Yes? Good … now, will you help Elise and Jason get these papers ready for distribution? Thank you."

Professional Characteristic Seven

*I demonstrate believably high levels of enthusiasm for
teaching/learning and for the content of my studies.*

My Current Level

1	2	3	4	5	6	7	8	9
(Not at all)								(At highest levels)

My Three-Year Goal

1	2	3	4	5	6	7	8	9
(Not at all)								(At highest levels)

My Estimate of Our Faculty Average

1	2	3	4	5	6	7	8	9
(Not at all)								(At highest levels)

My Estimate of Our Faculty Range (use brackets)

1	2	3	4	5	6	7	8	9
(Not at all)								(At highest levels)

Comment: This statement is *not* one that is made in reference to your "personality"
(an elusive concept in any case). The statement deals, rather, with the extent to which you
are able to give evidence—by your words and actions—to your students that (a) you are
eager for them to learn the material, (b) you are gratified when they do, and (c) you find the
content of your academic material of real (potential) significance to them. (Note: If your
"current level"—as reflected in the self-rating above—is quite low, this should serve as
a warning signal to you that, barring a meaningful experience of professional renewal, the
time may have come for you to retire or to move to another career.)

Professional Characteristic Eight

*I demonstrate through words and actions a genuine, believable commitment
to the school, its purposes, its leadership, and my peers.*

My Current Level

1	2	3	4	5	6	7	8	9
(Not at all)								*(At highest levels)*

My Three-Year Goal

1	2	3	4	5	6	7	8	9
(Not at all)								*(At highest levels)*

My Estimate of Our Faculty Average

1	2	3	4	5	6	7	8	9
(Not at all)								*(At highest levels)*

My Estimate of Our Faculty Range (use brackets)

1	2	3	4	5	6	7	8	9
(Not at all)								*(At highest levels)*

Comment: Your students' individual and collective commitments, or lack thereof, to your school, its purposes, and its personnel can be expected, in part, to reflect your own. Slighting verbal or nonverbal references on your part—in front of students—to the institution, its mission, or its people *will* influence students' attitudes and behaviors (and thus, their performance, satisfaction, and enthusiasm). This item is a "pure" *professional* characteristic. To fail here is not merely to fall short in areas of recommended instructional approaches, but to behave in ways that are actually unprofessional. There are consequences for the *students*.

Professional Characteristic Nine

I am glad to arrive at school and to see my students each day.

My Current Level

1	2	3	4	5	6	7	8	9
(Not at all)								(At highest levels)

My Three-Year Goal

1	2	3	4	5	6	7	8	9
(Not at all)								(At highest levels)

My Estimate of Our Faculty Average

1	2	3	4	5	6	7	8	9
(Not at all)								(At highest levels)

My Estimate of Our Faculty Range (use brackets)

1	2	3	4	5	6	7	8	9
(Not at all)								(At highest levels)

Comment: A teacher displaying the opposite of this characteristic will not *necessarily* appear angry, surly, or sullen upon her or his daily arrival at school. (No school employee consistently displaying those qualities will be long employed.) The "real-life" opposite of this characteristic describes a teacher who arrives at school appearing consistently listless, morose, or distracted. These qualities are translated by students—often correctly—as suggesting the teacher's lack of enthusiasm not merely for teaching as a meaningful activity, but that teacher's lack of enthusiasm for the students themselves. As with the previous item, your conduct and your demeanor have consequences for *student* performance, satisfaction, and enthusiasm.

Professional Characteristic Ten

I create predictable tests (not to be confused either with "simple" tests or with "easy" tests). My students can rely on the test preparation that I offer them.

My Current Level

1	2	3	4	5	6	7	8	9
(Not at all)								(At highest levels)

My Three-Year Goal

1	2	3	4	5	6	7	8	9
(Not at all)								(At highest levels)

My Estimate of Our Faculty Average

1	2	3	4	5	6	7	8	9
(Not at all)								(At highest levels)

My Estimate of Our Faculty Range (use brackets)

1	2	3	4	5	6	7	8	9
(Not at all)								(At highest levels)

Comment: This statement emphasizes the principle that tests of any sort should reveal each student's grasp of facts, concepts, and/or their applications in problem-solving contexts, *not* their abilities either to guess what the teacher means, to deal with unexpected testing formats, or to retrieve material that was not cited in assignments or in the test-review process. One of the surest ways to reduce levels of student performance, satisfaction, and enthusiasm is to test students in ways that leave them consistently feeling "tricked." Students should feel, upon receiving their grade, that they had been told what testing format to expect, what material would be covered, and something about the teacher's expectations (see Professional Characteristic No. 3, "Comment"). While authentic assessments that require students to demonstrate learned skills in new contexts can be excellent learning tools, students should know ahead of time that they will be asked to do this (if the context itself is not known), and they should have had plenty of low-stakes practice applying skills to new contexts prior to the graded assessment.

Professional Characteristic Eleven

I provide fair, reliable, understandable grade/reward structures for my students.
My students are led to understand why they receive the grades they receive—good
or bad—and thereby to see how improvement, if they will seek it, might be possible.

My Current Level

1	*2*	*3*	*4*	*5*	*6*	*7*	*8*	*9*
(Not at all)								*(At highest levels)*

My Three-Year Goal

1	*2*	*3*	*4*	*5*	*6*	*7*	*8*	*9*
(Not at all)								*(At highest levels)*

My Estimate of Our Faculty Average

1	*2*	*3*	*4*	*5*	*6*	*7*	*8*	*9*
(Not at all)								*(At highest levels)*

My Estimate of Our Faculty Range (use brackets)

1	*2*	*3*	*4*	*5*	*6*	*7*	*8*	*9*
(Not at all)								*(At highest levels)*

Comment: While the words "fair," "reliable," and "understandable" connote this Professional Characteristic's transparent relationship to "predictability," its relationship to "supportiveness" is even more critical. The simplest way to say this is that your feedback to your students on anything that is graded should leave them feeling *hopeful* that improvement might be possible. Your explicit comments—written or oral—on the steps needed to improve are considerably more important than the grade itself in this process. While the "improvement ball" always remains in your students' court, so to speak, the teacher's role must always include further instructions on the grip, the swing, the tactics, and the strategy. The least *and* the most academically gifted of your students must feel an unquestioning confidence that you expect them to get better, from the first day of school to the last.

Professional Characteristic Twelve

I enforce our rules, including the dress code, justly, fairly, consistently.

My Current Level

I	2	3	4	5	6	7	8	9
(Not at all)								(At highest levels)

My Three-Year Goal

I	2	3	4	5	6	7	8	9
(Not at all)								(At highest levels)

My Estimate of Our Faculty Average

I	2	3	4	5	6	7	8	9
(Not at all)								(At highest levels)

My Estimate of Our Faculty Range (use brackets)

I	2	3	4	5	6	7	8	9
(Not at all)								(At highest levels)

Comment: You may wish to review the "Comment" under Professional Characteristic No. 4. That characteristic dealt with setting specific behavioral expectations and standards for your own students in your own classroom, i.e., expectations and standards that promote your particular approach to the teaching/learning equation. Professional Characteristic No. 12, on the other hand, deals with schoolwide rules for behavior and appearance. You must be as "predictable" vis-à-vis these rules as with your own teaching/learning-specific ones. As noted in No. 4's "Comment," it is a fact that "bad laws make hard cases." When you are saddled with "bad laws" (i.e., schoolwide rules that strike you and/or your students as arbitrary and/or unnecessary), you cannot pretend they do not exist, nor can you attend to them selectively. Beyond individual consistency, it is important that **all** teachers apply the same rules in the same way. If one teacher negatively reinforces a behavior that another overlooks, a culture perceived as "unfair" by both students and teachers can develop

Professional Characteristic Thirteen

I am able to present myself each day in ways that will be seen by my students as consistent and reliable (i.e., unaffected by outside-of-school problems).

My Current Level

1	2	3	4	5	6	7	8	9
(Not at all)								(At highest levels)

My Three-Year Goal

1	2	3	4	5	6	7	8	9
(Not at all)								(At highest levels)

My Estimate of Our Faculty Average

1	2	3	4	5	6	7	8	9
(Not at all)								(At highest levels)

My Estimate of Our Faculty Range (use brackets)

1	2	3	4	5	6	7	8	9
(Not at all)								(At highest levels)

Comment: There are times when this characteristic will pose the supreme challenge. There are two "laws" to observe (1) if the issues are so weighty that you cannot rise above them while with your students, stay home; and (2) do *not* attempt to gain sympathy from students by sharing your issues with them in detail. You may find—or have already found—that going through your regular school day thoroughly focused on your students and on the teaching/learning process is, in itself, an effective method of coping with outside-of-school issues. But however you may choose to approach this situation, your job is to be "the same" person—in terms of your demeanor, your concentration, your enthusiasm, your dedication—each day, regardless of events in your personal life. Students must be able to count on the emotional and behavioral steadiness of their instructors. Their own lives are filled with uncertainties. You must not become an additional one.

Notes:

Self-Directed Analysis (Part Two)

The pages in this chapter will present—in the same self-rating format as the items in Chapter Two—a second tier of professional characteristics. These are "second tier" in the sense that they more closely parallel the findings of the original six-year ISM research project on the student experience than the findings from the more recent project. These second-tier items in no way contradict or detract from the 13 more recently developed items. They enrich and embellish them, but *they are not statistically tied as closely to student performance, student satisfaction, and student enthusiasm as the characteristics shown in Chapter Two.*

Said another way, these 22 second-tier items relate strongly to the original 20 principles for teaching excellence and, as well, to the original Faculty Culture Profile. (A list showing the "Twenty Principles for Teaching Excellence," exactly as they appeared in the ISM book by that title, can be viewed in Appendix D of this book.)

As you did with the items in Chapter Two, you should use the pages following as a workbook. Respond to the rating scales that are provided, make notes in the margins, converse about the items with your peers. Four rating scales are provided for each of the 22 characteristics. You may choose to respond only to the first scale in each case (the one referring to your current approach).

The other scales will allow you to record:

1. your aspirations,

2. your entire faculty's "averaged" ratings (in your own estimation), and

3. your entire faculty's *range* of approaches (again, of course, in your own estimation).

The scale is one through nine; nine is "high" on each item.

Note: Appendix F shows these same Characteristics of Professional Excellence in a format designed for use as a component in your faculty evaluation system, thereby connecting your faculty evaluation approach to student performance, satisfaction, and enthusiasm. When used in that context, you would rate yourself on each item, compare your self-ratings with your faculty supervisor's ratings of you, and use that (annual) conversation as a basis for continuing along your career-long professional development pathway.

Professional Characteristic Fourteen

I pursue career-long professional development as a foremost priority.

My Current Level

1	2	3	4	5	6	7	8	9
(Not at all)								(At highest levels)

My Three-Year Goal

1	2	3	4	5	6	7	8	9
(Not at all)								(At highest levels)

My Estimate of Our Faculty Average

1	2	3	4	5	6	7	8	9
(Not at all)								(At highest levels)

My Estimate of Our Faculty Range (use brackets)

1	2	3	4	5	6	7	8	9
(Not at all)								(At highest levels)

Professional Characteristic Fifteen

I am knowledgeable of cutting-edge content and developmental theory.

My Current Level

1	2	3	4	5	6	7	8	9
(Not at all)								(At highest levels)

My Three-Year Goal

1	2	3	4	5	6	7	8	9
(Not at all)								(At highest levels)

My Estimate of Our Faculty Average

1	2	3	4	5	6	7	8	9
(Not at all)								(At highest levels)

My Estimate of Our Faculty Range (use brackets)

1	2	3	4	5	6	7	8	9
(Not at all)								(At highest levels)

Professional Characteristic Sixteen

*I have mastered at least one pedagogical approach that is
supported by reliable, contemporary research outcomes.*

My Current Level

1	2	3	4	5	6	7	8	9

(Not at all)   (At highest levels)

My Three-Year Goal

1	2	3	4	5	6	7	8	9

(Not at all)   (At highest levels)

My Estimate of Our Faculty Average

1	2	3	4	5	6	7	8	9

(Not at all)   (At highest levels)

My Estimate of Our Faculty Range (use brackets)

1	2	3	4	5	6	7	8	9

(Not at all)   (At highest levels)

Professional Characteristic Seventeen

*I am practiced in establishing meaningful emotional/
psychological engagement with all my students.*

My Current Level

1	2	3	4	5	6	7	8	9
(Not at all)								(At highest levels)

My Three-Year Goal

1	2	3	4	5	6	7	8	9
(Not at all)								(At highest levels)

My Estimate of Our Faculty Average

1	2	3	4	5	6	7	8	9
(Not at all)								(At highest levels)

My Estimate of Our Faculty Range (use brackets)

1	2	3	4	5	6	7	8	9
(Not at all)								(At highest levels)

Professional Characteristic Eighteen

*I am practiced in finding creative and appropriate ways
to be involved with my students outside the classroom.*

My Current Level

1	2	3	4	5	6	7	8	9
(Not at all)								(At highest levels)

My Three-Year Goal

1	2	3	4	5	6	7	8	9
(Not at all)								(At highest levels)

My Estimate of Our Faculty Average

1	2	3	4	5	6	7	8	9
(Not at all)								(At highest levels)

My Estimate of Our Faculty Range (use brackets)

1	2	3	4	5	6	7	8	9
(Not at all)								(At highest levels)

Professional Characteristic Nineteen

I am practiced in displaying an overt, conspicuous interest in students' outside-the-classroom lives—apart from the previous item—without crossing privacy barriers.

My Current Level

1	2	3	4	5	6	7	8	9
(Not at all)								(At highest levels)

My Three-Year Goal

1	2	3	4	5	6	7	8	9
(Not at all)								(At highest levels)

My Estimate of Our Faculty Average

1	2	3	4	5	6	7	8	9
(Not at all)								(At highest levels)

My Estimate of Our Faculty Range (use brackets)

1	2	3	4	5	6	7	8	9
(Not at all)								(At highest levels)

Professional Characteristic Twenty

I am practiced in applying any subject matter to real-life conditions beyond the classroom, including applications that may be global or universal in their potential.

My Current Level

1	2	3	4	5	6	7	8	9

(Not at all)   *(At highest levels)*

My Three-Year Goal

1	2	3	4	5	6	7	8	9

(Not at all)   *(At highest levels)*

My Estimate of Our Faculty Average

1	2	3	4	5	6	7	8	9

(Not at all)   *(At highest levels)*

My Estimate of Our Faculty Range (use brackets)

1	2	3	4	5	6	7	8	9

(Not at all)   *(At highest levels)*

Professional Characteristic Twenty-One

*I am practiced in providing private and public positive
reinforcement for individual or group (student) successes.*

My Current Level

1	2	3	4	5	6	7	8	9
(Not at all)								(At highest levels)

My Three-Year Goal

1	2	3	4	5	6	7	8	9
(Not at all)								(At highest levels)

My Estimate of Our Faculty Average

1	2	3	4	5	6	7	8	9
(Not at all)								(At highest levels)

My Estimate of Our Faculty Range (use brackets)

1	2	3	4	5	6	7	8	9
(Not at all)								(At highest levels)

Professional Characteristic Twenty-Two

I am practiced in giving active support for, and establishing active engagement with, my colleagues.

My Current Level

| 1 | 2 | 3 | 4 | 5 | 6 | 7 | 8 | 9 |

(Not at all)   (At highest levels)

My Three-Year Goal

| 1 | 2 | 3 | 4 | 5 | 6 | 7 | 8 | 9 |

(Not at all)   (At highest levels)

My Estimate of Our Faculty Average

| 1 | 2 | 3 | 4 | 5 | 6 | 7 | 8 | 9 |

(Not at all)   (At highest levels)

My Estimate of Our Faculty Range (use brackets)

| 1 | 2 | 3 | 4 | 5 | 6 | 7 | 8 | 9 |

(Not at all)   (At highest levels)

Professional Characteristic Twenty-Three

I am practiced in making positive contributions to a professional, mission-focused sense of community with all constituent groups.

My Current Level

1	2	3	4	5	6	7	8	9
(Not at all)								(At highest levels)

My Three-Year Goal

1	2	3	4	5	6	7	8	9
(Not at all)								(At highest levels)

My Estimate of Our Faculty Average

1	2	3	4	5	6	7	8	9
(Not at all)								(At highest levels)

My Estimate of Our Faculty Range (use brackets)

1	2	3	4	5	6	7	8	9
(Not at all)								(At highest levels)

Professional Characteristic Twenty-Four

I am practiced in establishing proactive communication with, and service to, each student's parents.

My Current Level

1	2	3	4	5	6	7	8	9
(Not at all)								(At highest levels)

My Three-Year Goal

1	2	3	4	5	6	7	8	9
(Not at all)								(At highest levels)

My Estimate of Our Faculty Average

1	2	3	4	5	6	7	8	9
(Not at all)								(At highest levels)

My Estimate of Our Faculty Range (use brackets)

1	2	3	4	5	6	7	8	9
(Not at all)								(At highest levels)

Professional Characteristic Twenty-Five

I am practiced in making an overt commitment to the personal and professional well-being of my colleagues, of my administrators, and of (other) nonteaching staff.

My Current Level

1	2	3	4	5	6	7	8	9
(Not at all)								(At highest levels)

My Three-Year Goal

1	2	3	4	5	6	7	8	9
(Not at all)								(At highest levels)

My Estimate of Our Faculty Average

1	2	3	4	5	6	7	8	9
(Not at all)								(At highest levels)

My Estimate of Our Faculty Range (use brackets)

1	2	3	4	5	6	7	8	9
(Not at all)								(At highest levels)

Professional Characteristic Twenty-Six

*I am practiced in giving public support for my students,
my colleagues, and my employers (administration and Board).*

My Current Level

I	2	3	4	5	6	7	8	9
(Not at all)								(At highest levels)

My Three-Year Goal

I	2	3	4	5	6	7	8	9
(Not at all)								(At highest levels)

My Estimate of Our Faculty Average

I	2	3	4	5	6	7	8	9
(Not at all)								(At highest levels)

My Estimate of Our Faculty Range (use brackets)

I	2	3	4	5	6	7	8	9
(Not at all)								(At highest levels)

Professional Characteristic Twenty-Seven

I am practiced in communicating in-class experimentation-and-testing outcomes and findings to colleagues within and beyond the school.

My Current Level

1	2	3	4	5	6	7	8	9

(Not at all)   (At highest levels)

My Three-Year Goal

1	2	3	4	5	6	7	8	9

(Not at all)   (At highest levels)

My Estimate of Our Faculty Average

1	2	3	4	5	6	7	8	9

(Not at all)   (At highest levels)

My Estimate of Our Faculty Range (use brackets)

1	2	3	4	5	6	7	8	9

(Not at all)   (At highest levels)

Professional Characteristic Twenty-Eight

I am practiced in routine (yet enthusiastic) participation in outside-the-school academic organizations whose work is supportive of, and pertinent to, my field(s).

My Current Level

1	2	3	4	5	6	7	8	9

(Not at all)   (At highest levels)

My Three-Year Goal

1	2	3	4	5	6	7	8	9

(Not at all)   (At highest levels)

My Estimate of Our Faculty Average

1	2	3	4	5	6	7	8	9

(Not at all)   (At highest levels)

My Estimate of Our Faculty Range (use brackets)

1	2	3	4	5	6	7	8	9

(Not at all)   (At highest levels)

(Items 29–35 pertain to schools with religious missions)

Professional Characteristic Twenty-Nine

I am practiced in making an overt commitment to the life of my own congregation (church, synagogue, etc.) and its core traditions.

My Current Level

1	2	3	4	5	6	7	8	9
(Not at all)								*(At highest levels)*

My Three-Year Goal

1	2	3	4	5	6	7	8	9
(Not at all)								*(At highest levels)*

My Estimate of Our Faculty Average

1	2	3	4	5	6	7	8	9
(Not at all)								*(At highest levels)*

My Estimate of Our Faculty Range (use brackets)

1	2	3	4	5	6	7	8	9
(Not at all)								*(At highest levels)*

Professional Characteristic Thirty

I am practiced in serving as a mature role model for a biblically observant lifestyle.

My Current Level

1	2	3	4	5	6	7	8	9
(Not at all)								*(At highest levels)*

My Three-Year Goal

1	2	3	4	5	6	7	8	9
(Not at all)								*(At highest levels)*

My Estimate of Our Faculty Average

1	2	3	4	5	6	7	8	9
(Not at all)								*(At highest levels)*

My Estimate of Our Faculty Range (use brackets)

1	2	3	4	5	6	7	8	9
(Not at all)								*(At highest levels)*

Professional Characteristic Thirty-One

I am skilled in articulating the personal/ethical implications of a lifelong faith commitment.

My Current Level

1	2	3	4	5	6	7	8	9
(Not at all)								(At highest levels)

My Three-Year Goal

1	2	3	4	5	6	7	8	9
(Not at all)								(At highest levels)

My Estimate of Our Faculty Average

1	2	3	4	5	6	7	8	9
(Not at all)								(At highest levels)

My Estimate of Our Faculty Range (use brackets)

1	2	3	4	5	6	7	8	9
(Not at all)								(At highest levels)

Professional Characteristic Thirty-Two

I am practiced in displaying appropriate levels of public tolerance of, and respect for, other religious points of view.

My Current Level

1	2	3	4	5	6	7	8	9
(Not at all)								(At highest levels)

My Three-Year Goal

1	2	3	4	5	6	7	8	9
(Not at all)								(At highest levels)

My Estimate of Our Faculty Average

1	2	3	4	5	6	7	8	9
(Not at all)								(At highest levels)

My Estimate of Our Faculty Range (use brackets)

1	2	3	4	5	6	7	8	9
(Not at all)								(At highest levels)

Professional Characteristic Thirty-Three

I am knowledgeable of the developmental history of my school's religious heritage.

My Current Level

1	2	3	4	5	6	7	8	9
(Not at all)								(At highest levels)

My Three-Year Goal

1	2	3	4	5	6	7	8	9
(Not at all)								(At highest levels)

My Estimate of Our Faculty Average

1	2	3	4	5	6	7	8	9
(Not at all)								(At highest levels)

My Estimate of Our Faculty Range (use brackets)

1	2	3	4	5	6	7	8	9
(Not at all)								(At highest levels)

Professional Characteristic Thirty-Four

I am practiced in participating in (and when appropriate, leading) the
explicitly religious components of the school's student and community programs.

My Current Level

1	2	3	4	5	6	7	8	9

(Not at all)   (At highest levels)

My Three-Year Goal

1	2	3	4	5	6	7	8	9

(Not at all)   (At highest levels)

My Estimate of Our Faculty Average

1	2	3	4	5	6	7	8	9

(Not at all)   (At highest levels)

My Estimate of Our Faculty Range (use brackets)

1	2	3	4	5	6	7	8	9

(Not at all)   (At highest levels)

Professional Characteristic Thirty-Five

*I am committed to growing professionally and personally
within the framework of my religious traditions.*

My Current Level

1	2	3	4	5	6	7	8	9
(Not at all)								*(At highest levels)*

My Three-Year Goal

1	2	3	4	5	6	7	8	9
(Not at all)								*(At highest levels)*

My Estimate of Our Faculty Average

1	2	3	4	5	6	7	8	9
(Not at all)								*(At highest levels)*

My Estimate of Our Faculty Range (use brackets)

1	2	3	4	5	6	7	8	9
(Not at all)								*(At highest levels)*

Notes:

Teachers as Leaders

Many of the most high-impact professional characteristics of teachers (those whose approaches are associated with high levels of student performance, satisfaction, and enthusiasm) are also characteristics found in common with contemporary views of good leadership.

What are some of those characteristics? They may include:

- knowledge and expertise, which are readily perceived (*by followers*);
- a drive to stay "current" in relevant fields;
- repeatedly articulated (*to followers*) standards for performance and conduct;
- a "results" orientation;
- a "vision" of the process and the end product (and the ability and willingness to describe that vision *to followers*, often and well);
- a facility for infusing routine activities with meaning;
- a passion for preparation;
- flexibility, especially in design and evaluation;
- humaneness (as perceived *by followers*);
- a knack for confronting without being demeaning;
- the ability to teach (not merely assign) "responsibility"; and
- constant attention to reinforcement principles (feedback).

These ideas are not different from many of the ones expressed by a number of the Characteristics of Professional Excellence as listed in the "Self-Directed Analysis" Chapters Two and Three. Many of these leadership characteristics represent sets of ideas identical to those in the aforementioned chapters, but usually couched in terms reserved for books and articles on leadership.

Are good leadership and good teaching "the same thing"? Not exactly. *But in those schools in which student performance/satisfaction/enthusiasm levels are strong, teaching approaches in general are strikingly consistent with recognized "good leadership" characteristics.*

The late John W. Gardner, preeminent author and role model in the field, has written that those in leadership too often think that their position on the organizational chart gives them a body of "followers" (in this case, of "students") in more than name only. In fact, Gardner notes, leaders' organizational positions only give them "subordinates." These subordinates may or may not become followers, depending upon whether or not their leaders become leaders. (Most of these thoughts closely parallel discussions he contributed to *Leadership: An Overview,* one of a series of papers prepared for the Leadership Studies Program sponsored by Independent Sector.)

Leadership, Gardner noted, is not the same as status, power, or authority. It is a process of organizing, persuading, and exemplifying that ultimately results in creation or modification of followers' knowledge, behaviors, attitudes, and habits. Leaders bestow psychological rewards—positive and negative reinforcement—*in such a way as to increase followers' sense of hope, confidence, and belief in the efficacy of their own efforts*. Above all, leaders set conditions within their own organizations that foster a sense of continuous renewal.

Reflect on your current teaching situation. To what extent are your in-class imperfections and difficulties a result of your assuming that your status, that of teacher, gives you "followers"? Several examples of *not* holding that assumption—examples of "good teacher/leader behavior"— follow. You will find an example from each of three levels—lower, middle, and upper school.

1. **Lower-school teacher Jones** understands that eliciting the highest (realistically attainable) performance from her students will necessitate "converting" not only her students but her students' parents, as well, to her views on third-graders' goals, standards, and expectations. To accomplish that, she must be convincing in front of the children and, beyond that, actually demonstrate—in person, by phone, and/or in e-mails— to their parents that she is:

   – broadly knowledgeable, astute, and academically current, ideally via actual face-to-face meetings with the children's parents;

   – articulate regarding a set of clear and exciting (to students and parents) expectations for these children's progress during this school year;

   – articulate regarding a set of clear and realistic expectations of the students' parents' roles in assisting the children in meeting her expectations for each child in her class, a set of expectations that will include written guidelines, procedures, and objectives for the parents;

   – *personally excited by, visibly passionate about, and unswervingly committed* to helping these children experience a daily sense of accomplishment that is grounded in *real progress* (as distinct from the students' being led to "feel good about themselves" as an emotional status independent of such real progress); and

   – kind, humane, and supportive both of children and parents, a leader who can and who obviously does empathize with her two sets of followers.

2. **Middle-school teacher Escobar** understands that eliciting the highest (realistically attainable) performance from each of his students will require him to achieve a finely adjusted balance between these young people's overwhelming need to be treated "like adults" and their bouncing-off-the-walls volatility. To find and maintain that balance, he will need to:

– master the art of confronting-without-demeaning, and *expect to practice that art daily*;

– demonstrate his presumably considerable subject-area(s) mastery in ways that simultaneously impress the young people and honor their (self-described) adult-like mental capacities;

– pour huge amounts of time into preparation *in order to achieve flexibility* (rather than in order to achieve rigidity) in his daily instructional designs, thereby maintaining the ability to *lead* in a well-planned way in any of several directions, even during a single class period;

– integrate into that preparation time effective ways of "making the routine meaningful" to pubescent human beings, partly by articulating and embodying the honest excitement he has for his field and partly by utilizing choice-within-structure classroom techniques; and,

– attend with special care to his "results orientation" by means of regular, carefully articulated statements and written reminders of the expectations he has formulated for each student by year-end.

3. **Upper-school teacher Kandahar** understands that inspiring the highest (realistically attainable) performance from her students will require focused attention to content and theory in her academic field(s), coupled with a strong dose in equal measure of these psychologically difficult-to-combine conditions: high standards and difficult-to-reach goals for the students, on the one hand, and powerful instructional and personal support for the students as they work toward those goals, on the other. In working to establish these conditions, she will need to:

– demonstrate the currency of her expertise and knowledge, citing this year's groundbreaking development in her field, this month's published report, yesterday's news release;

– couple that demonstrating-of-expertise with an oft-stated "leaderly vision" of the future, both for developments in her field, and for her students (as those developments hold potential for their futures)—for example, envisioning for and with her students the implications of 21st century technology for language-learning, for written communication, for mathematical computation and application, for physics/engineering, for electronics/engineering, for organizational structure and opportunity, for parenting and family life, for the "schooling" process at all levels; and

– avoid "front-and-center teaching/leading" as her primary *modus operandi*, thereby acknowledging in her teaching/leading approach that in high-performing classrooms the students' time-on-task (writing, computing, creating, discussing, planning) must outweigh the teacher's time-in-lecture (not to suggest that front-and-center teaching/leading should *necessarily* be reduced to a mere fraction of total in-class time, but that it should consistently total less than 50%).

The three examples just given are only that—examples. They illustrate some of the steps which teachers at various levels may consider taking in response to the 13 Professional Characteristics shown and commented upon in Chapter Two and the 22 second-tier Professional Characteristics listed in Chapter Three.

Notes:

Followship: Learned Optimism and True Grit

As noted in the previous chapter, a leadership position (such as that of faculty member) does not automatically give one "followers"; it gives one "subordinates." Subordinates (i.e., students) become followers (i.e., learners) if superiors (i.e., faculty members) become leaders (i.e., teachers).

This chapter's title highlights leadership attitudes/behaviors of the sort that generate "followship" responses in students that tend to conform to a set of concepts originating in Dr. Martin Seligman's theories. These theories have also been used as a springboard to related research and formulations by many scholars and practitioners, notably Dr. Angela Duckworth. (Martin Seligman's seminal ideas can be reviewed in his classic work *Learned Optimism* and, even earlier, his *Psychopathology: Experimental Models*. Dr. Seligman is the author of the former; he edited and contributed to the latter. Angela Duckworth's innumerable publications include "Temperament in the Classroom," *Handbook of Temperament*, pp. 627–644.)

When applied to classrooms, Seligman's concepts imply that a teacher's response to a student will move that student toward "learned helplessness" or, alternatively, toward "learned optimism," depending upon the response's characteristics and the tendencies of the student. When students see no connection between what they attempt and the apparent result, their mind-sets tend toward "learned helplessness." Conversely, when students do see connections between what they attempt and the result, their mind-sets tend toward "learned optimism."

Learned helplessness is associated with lack of persistence and lack of determination (because there is no point in persisting when effort does not connect—in the student's mind—to outcomes). Learned optimism is associated with high levels of both persistence and determination, and, thus, with resilience (because the student believes that continued effort will eventually bring positive results).

Angela Duckworth's concept of "grit" layers itself nicely into the learned helplessness/learned optimism framework. She has found that grit ranks among the prime determinants of student success (ahead, in some contexts, even of intelligence). She defines grit as "sticking with things ... until you master them."

For the teacher, the key question about both learned optimism and grit is *Can these characteristics be taught and learned?* And the answer is *Yes, they can.* The trick is to provide students with such consistent and reliable reinforcement—positive or negative, as each instance merits, moment-to-moment—that they begin routinely to connect what they do with the (psychological) reward that their teacher(s) provides.

A number of the Professional Characteristics cited in Chapters Two and Three have particular relevance. Several of them are repeated on the following pages.

Review each of these concepts, bearing in mind "learned optimism" and "gritty determination." Imagine how these teacher/leader behaviors might act on students, first to generate, and then draw out, the critical student characteristics of learned optimism (*the expectation that effort will reliably connect to result*) and grit (*the settled determination to stick with things until they are mastered.*)

Professional Characteristic Three: *I set clearly articulated standards for student academic performance.*

Comment: This is a statement not about your own scoring and grading system itself, but about your ability and willingness to illuminate the nature of your academic expectations, i.e., not about explaining that 90–93 = A- and 94–97 = A and 98–100 = A+, but delineating (in age-appropriate fashion, of course) the subject-specific levels of mastery that you expect from your students. An illustration of this might entail: providing students with examples (in advance of an assignment) of submissions that you would grade as A, B, C, and so on, or involving your students in the development of the rubric.

Professional Characteristic Ten: *I create predictable tests (not to be confused either with "simple" tests or with "easy" tests). My students can rely on the test preparation that I offer them.*

Comment: This statement emphasizes the principle that tests of any sort should reveal each student's grasp of facts, concepts, and/or their applications in problem-solving contexts, *not* their abilities either to guess what the teacher means, to deal with unexpected testing formats, or to retrieve material that was not cited in assignments or in the test-review process. One of the surest ways to reduce levels of student performance, satisfaction, and enthusiasm is to test students in ways that leave them consistently feeling "tricked." Students should feel, upon receiving their grade, that they had been told what testing format to expect, what material would be covered, and something about the teacher's expectations (see Professional Characteristic No. 3, "Comment"). While authentic assessments that require students to demonstrate learned skills in new contexts can be excellent learning tools, students should know ahead of time that they will be asked to do this (if the context itself is not known). They should have had plenty of low-stakes practice applying skills to new contexts prior to the graded assessment.

Professional Characteristic Eleven: *I provide fair, reliable, understandable grade/reward structures for my students. My students are led to understand why they receive the grades they receive—good or bad—and thereby to see how improvement, if they will seek it, might be possible.*

Comment: While the words "fair," "reliable," and "understandable" connote this Professional Characteristic's transparent relationship to "predictability," its relationship to "supportiveness" is even more critical. The simplest way to say this is that your feedback to your students on anything that is graded should leave them feeling *hopeful* that improvement might be possible. Your explicit comments—written or oral—on the steps needed to improve are considerably more important than the grade itself in this process. While the "improvement ball" always remains in your students' court, so to speak, the teacher's role must always include further instructions on the grip, the swing, the tactics, and the strategy. The least *and* the most academically gifted of your students must feel an unquestioning confidence that you expect them to get better, from the first day of school to the last.

Among other first-tier (Chapter Two) characteristics, you may wish to review:

Professional Characteristic One: *I find ways to make it obvious to all students that I wish them success every day, both in school and outside of school.*

Professional Characteristic Seven: *I demonstrate believably high levels of enthusiasm for teaching/learning and for the content of my studies*

Among the second-tier (Chapter Three) characteristics, you may wish to review:

Professional Characteristic Seventeen: *I am practiced in establishing meaningful emotional/ psychological engagement with all my students.*

Professional Characteristic Twenty-One: *I am practiced in providing private and public positive reinforcement for individual or group (student) successes.*

Now, having reviewed this smattering of the most pertinent Chapter Two and Chapter Three Professional Characteristics, consider several classroom-specific examples as viewed through the student lens.

Suppose you are a ninth-grader, and suppose you submit an essay and form an expectation somehow that it is worth about a "B." It comes back a "C." The teacher's only written comments are (in your mind) vague and unhelpful (e.g., "Good effort, but slightly unfocused"). *You see no obvious connection between what you tried to do and the apparent result.* Learned helplessness has just been reinforced. Persistence (and thus performance, satisfaction, and enthusiasm) will begin to diminish.

If you, the student, are "gritty" enough, you may have to endure many such unexplained disappointments before these characteristics—performance/satisfaction/enthusiasm—begin to diminish. If you, the student, are not particularly "gritty," the onset of this decline may come fairly soon.

Note that it is *not* an issue of being given a grade that is lower than you hoped for, or expected, that has the debilitating influence on your future performance. Rather, it is *not having the teacher's rationale for the grade explained at all—or in a way that you can understand—that initiates the insidious decline.*

Now suppose you that you are a third-grader and that you decide to construct for your quarterly science project a diorama of the Colorado River's course, using a shoe box and clay. You bring it to school and your diorama takes its place among 20 other student projects. Your teacher gives blue ribbons to three of the projects. Yours is not one of them. Your science grade for the quarter is a "C." *You see no obvious connection between what you tried to do and the apparent result.* Learned helplessness has just been reinforced. Persistence (and thus performance, satisfaction, and enthusiasm) will begin to diminish.

Again, the issue is not the mediocre quality of your diorama. The issue is your teacher's having not taken the time to explain to you what exactly was good and not-so-good about your project. Words such as these can do wonders: "Next time, if you will try doing such-and-such, rather than such-and-such, I would expect your project to turn out quite nicely." (Please note the absence of any guarantee or promise of a better grade, but, rather, the simple commentary on the project's strengths and weaknesses, coupled with the forward view to something that might turn out better next time.)

Examples abound: You, as a student, come to class ten minutes late and no negative reinforcement is forthcoming. You, as a student, do not prepare for your chemistry quiz, but your grade is as good as usual. You, as a student, *do* prepare with extraordinary care (by your own standards) for your math exam, but your grade, though improved in its raw score, is still the usual "C" (because your classmates in general did better, too, and because the math teacher chose to "grade on the curve").

In each of these instances, you, the student, see no obvious connection between what you tried to do (or failed to do) and the apparent result. Learned helplessness has been reinforced. Persistence (and thus performance, satisfaction, and enthusiasm) will begin to diminish.

You, the teacher, hold the key to reversing this kind of deterioration. Note that the expected deterioration is not just in student performance. It is, as well, in student satisfaction with, and enthusiasm for, the schooling experience. Note, too, that this has nothing to do with whether you, as a teacher, are viewed as "hard" or "easy."

So, to elicit consistently high-level performance (in the context, of course, of each student's native capacity) in your students, regardless of their age or grade level, concentrate on the kind of thoroughgoing reinforcement that lets them know just where they are in your estimation at all times, academically and behaviorally. Inspire them to work for high-level goals and simultaneously provide them with the positive and/or negative reinforcement that will be necessary to help them get there.

The two caveats are (1) no "false positives"—no grade inflation solely "to make them feel good about themselves"—in your reinforcement, and (2) no instances of students being compared with each other (rather than with themselves over time).

In regard to the first caveat, this implies that students must *earn* your approval. Your challenge is to set up learning conditions so that they *can*, no matter how incrementally, experience some successes, whether large or small. But it is essential to withhold approval when it is not earned. Do not make the mistake of cheapening the value of your positive reinforcement.

The second caveat implies that students should be rewarded for their own individual improvement (against your standards), rather than being rewarded only when performance surpasses that of their peers. This second caveat, as with nearly all recommendations that appear in this book, pertains specifically to classroom teaching and its ancillary activities of supervision in hallways, in lunchrooms, in after-school programs, and so on. This is not meant to discourage all competitive activities. Sports, music competition, science competition, competition for scholarships, and so on, can contribute usefully—*if coached, directed, and managed appropriately*—to the mission-related value of the overall schooling experience.

Anticipation and Renewal

What was your original impetus toward teaching as a possible career? What excited you about the prospect? What did you imagine in your mind's eye when you thought of yourself actually teaching? What really provided the motivation to prepare yourself, to seek a position, and to invest huge amounts of your effort and time—and money—into beginning this career?

Regardless of your current "stage" of career, what has become of those impetus-generators? Are they still present, and in similar strength and proportion? Is your current reason-for-teaching compatible with the implications of the earlier chapters of this book? Will your current motivation be equal to the task of adopting these Professional Characteristics and working toward excellence on each?

Depending on the stage of each teacher's career, certain faculty members may demonstrate the following qualities:

- preoccupation with family and leisure activities—certainly not a bad thing in itself—coupled with (however) a turning away from career interests, excitement, and motivation;

- marked reduction in earlier excitement about the intrinsic rewards found in teaching and guiding young people;

- loss of the *learned optimism* experienced regularly when faculty members were first mastering the teaching art, when they were more impressed by and excited about the connections they had begun to perceive between what they tried to do and the results of those efforts; and

- a perception of reduced career opportunity, a sense that fewer options await them on their career journeys.

If any of this describes you personally or if you observe this in others within the faculty on which you serve, then give considerable thought to the implications of the "ISM School Culture Matrix," the four-quadrant diagram that appeared as "Figure 3" in Chapter One. The likelihood is that without an ongoing faculty-endorsed culture of renewal, everyone—students, teachers, support staff, and administration—is simply "less" as a result: less high-performing, less satisfied, and less enthusiastic.

This is your career. You either move your career forward, or it tends toward stagnation. You move it forward by (a) maintaining high levels of *interest* in your fields of expertise—reading in professional journals, discussing concepts and techniques with peers, engaging in periodic formal study of various kinds—and (b) maintaining high levels of *involvement* in the lives of your students.

You set goals for yourself in both categories: your academic expertise *and* your involvement with students. You move toward the goals. As you move toward them, you establish new ones. There is no limit to a teaching career's opportunities for learning. But more so than most careers, the career of the teacher is the prisoner of each individual teacher's own decisions about whether to let the career flourish or wither.

Renewal must become a fact of life in any organization for its individual and collective existence to become anything other than mundane. As a teacher, you will endeavor to make continuous learning a fact of life for your students.

What about for yourself? Consider some or all of the ideas/suggestions that follow, and/or invent your own set. Some deal with the short term; others, with the long term of your entire career.

- Does setting "clearly articulated standards for student academic performance" or demonstrating "believably high levels of enthusiasm ... for the content of my studies" (see Professional Characteristics No. 3 and 7 in Chapter Two) seem too much of a stretch at this stage of your career? What would happen if you arranged to observe (more than once) a colleague—on your faculty or on some other faculty—whose reputation for inspiring students in these ways is substantial?

- Is staying on the "cutting edge" too much trouble (see Professional Characteristics No. 14, 15, 16, 27, and 28 in Chapter Three)? What would happen if you and several colleagues formed a "Mathematics Breakfast Club" or an "After-hours (Children's) Literature Study" or an every-faculty-meeting "Reading Theory Colloquium"?

- Do increased levels of outside-of-class involvement with students (see Professional Characteristics No. 18 and 19 in Chapter Three) strike you as a heinous burden? What would happen if you initiated something on your own terms? For example, rather than volunteering to coordinate the next field trip—something requiring months of planning—suppose you offered to conduct periodic after-school or evening sessions on something in which you have both interest and informal expertise, say, Meteorology or Nutrition or Behavioral Health? Bear in mind that "involvement" is the operative word. Making a *presentation* periodically probably would not fit. Scraping together half-dozen inexpensive telescopes periodically and chatting with students and parents about planets and stars and galaxies certainly would.

- Consider crafting at least the outline of a career-long professional development plan. The plan should include formal study in your field(s) at least every 36–48 months. This can be for graduate credit or not for graduate credit, but it should, above all, be *interesting, meaningful, and exciting to you*. Otherwise, do not bother. "Credit" and "meaning" are not necessarily related to each other.

- Your professional development plan should thoroughly and thoughtfully dovetail with the plans of at least one of your colleagues on your faculty. By coordinating these plans yourselves, you multiply your efforts. You learn from each other.

- Your professional development plan might benefit from a formal or informal *peer-renewal system*. This may or may not have anything to do with your administration's faculty evaluation system. (It is often difficult to combine the two in a formal way, since the peer renewal system has only one objective—*mutual* personal/professional renewal—while the administrative system often includes contracts and salaries in its objectives.)

- Your professional development plan should connect you with your original impetus for entering the teaching field. Often that original impetus was laced with idealism. *Recapture that, in some "more mature" version*. Your plan will display more realism and pragmatism than any plan you could have written earlier, no matter where you are now in your career development, but it should not ignore that seminal idealism which led you initially to the classroom.

- Your professional development plan should have self-rewards built into it. The further you develop in your profession, the less likely you are (in many schools) to receive positive reinforcement from your administration, no matter how excellent its members may be. Your competence becomes "assumed." So, rather than developing *learned helplessness* because you see no connection between your efforts and your administrators' acknowledgment of those efforts, build *self-reinforcement* into your *self-renewal* plan. Make sure you and your peers, for example, reinforce each other on a regular basis (but, as with the students, only when reinforcement is actually *earned*). Make sure your plan is written, so that you can monitor your progress in a formal way. And every time you attend a workshop or a course, make sure there is a tangible acknowledgment of that, e.g., a certificate which you post in a place routinely visible to you. (If the workshop gives none, make your own, and make it attractive.) Share what you learn through a workshop or course with your colleagues and request of your administrators that this be the expectation for all teachers.

Arrange your professional (and personal) life so that you can see the connections between your efforts and your efforts' outcomes. Learned optimism implies writing a career professional development plan, following that plan, and rewarding yourself systematically as you reach its various targets. The results for you are the same as the results for your students when you lead them to experience learned optimism: *persistence, performance, satisfaction, and enthusiasm*.

Notes:

Parenting—Home and School

The very best teachers have always parented. Regardless of their students' ages, they have parented. Regardless of their students' socioeconomic backgrounds, they have parented. Regardless of the subject matter, they have parented.

That is, the very best teachers have *engaged* their students in life-shaping ways and at life-changing levels. By example and by persuasion—overt or subtle—they have stamped their students with an unmistakable imprint: personal responsibility, maturity, integrity, loyalty.

This engaged-teacher role has been a critical one for countess students. That role threatens now to become yet more critical as the parent-at-home role diminishes.

Many students come from families with dual-working parents, single-parent families, and, in those families, the ubiquitous television sets and handheld electronic devices all busily "teaching" their own values, nonvalues, and antivalues. This often leaves teachers as collectively the best-positioned individuals in society to deliver those four classic parental values: personal responsibility, maturity, integrity, loyalty. The state of the family now implies that teachers, as a body of professionals, must consider this kind of classroom parenting a basic, indispensable component of their calling.

The concepts of "learned helplessness" and "learned optimism," as crucial factors in a given student's persistence, performance, satisfaction, and enthusiasm levels have been described at length throughout this workbook. Now consider those concepts in the context of the relationship between home and school.

If the at-home parents (as distinct from the teachers-as-parents) define "success" for their children only as perfection or as being "first," their reinforcement program will not match yours (provided you are using the Professional Characteristics recommended in Chapters Two and Three). You will be reinforcing incremental improvements demonstrated by the student, regardless of the student's distance from perfection or from "first place." In a student facing this contradiction, learned helplessness at home will compete with the learned optimism you are developing at school. The net impact on a given student's persistence, performance, satisfaction, and enthusiasm is not predictable.

Similarly, if the at-home parents (as distinct from the teachers-as-parents) are totally non-reinforcing, perhaps because they are more interested in being "friends" with their children than in guiding them, the two reinforcement programs again will not match. In the case of a given student facing this inconsistency, the net impact on that student's persistence, performance, satisfaction, and enthusiasm is not predictable, any more than in the first instance.

What does this imply? Simply that if you and your colleagues implement the Professional Characteristics advocated in this workbook at a level approaching true excellence, so learned optimism is rampant at your school, you *still* may lose some of your students to the counterbalancing forces of their at-home parents.

Angela Duckworth's concept of "gritty persistence" in your students exists, of course, as the other wild card which you can only influence, rather than control. No matter what you and your colleagues do, persistence, performance, satisfaction, and enthusiasm may still deteriorate in some of your students.

In lower-school, self-contained classrooms in which you are the teacher with whom your students spend most of every day, a Parent Education Plan (PEP)—whether devised by you alone for your students' parents or devised by your faculty-administration as a schoolwide effort—is potentially very significant. A PEP that communicates to parents in lay terms what you are trying to accomplish may help your students encounter mutually reinforcing strategies at home and at school.

Consider, for example, the implications within a PEP of Professional Characteristics such as No. 4 ("I set reasonable, defensible standards for student behavior") or No. 12 ("I enforce our rules, including the dress code, justly, fairly, consistently") or No. 13 ("I am able to present myself each day in ways that will be seen by my students as consistent and reliable, i.e., unaffected by outside-of-school problems") or No. 24 ("I am practiced in establishing proactive communication with, and service to, each student's parents"). Imagine a PEP that explicates and illustrates for your lower-school parents the meaning of such characteristics. Parents who choose private-independent schools for their children are usually (not always, of course) willing learners. Educate them. Give them the chance to reinforce these children at home with approaches similar to those you employ at school.

For middle- and upper-school students whose daily contact with you may be less than one hour (because of your departmentalized schedule), the importance of a faculty-wide approach becomes especially critical. A student who, for example, encounters but one teacher per day who utilizes the 13 Professional Characteristics spelled out in Chapter Two of this workbook, and who then faces five who do not (and, as well, a set of at-home parents who also do not) would need to have a stunning measure of Duckworth's "gritty" determination to maintain consistent performance, strong levels of satisfaction, and genuine enthusiasm, no matter what you—acting alone—are able to do.

But if a given student, hour-after-hour, day-after-day, and year-after-year, encounters a unified faculty culture that reinforces in her or him the development of learning habits and behavioral responses consistent with this workbook's Professional Characteristics, the chances of counterbalancing nonsupportive at-home parenting may change from marginal to good. And if, through an appropriate schoolwide PEP, parental support is enlisted for the entire endeavor, the percentage of learned-helpless students in your school can be expected to be small indeed.

Notes:

Revisiting Your Academic Roots

Think back.

Try to remember your first true experience of *intellectual* excitement.

Was it rooted in dinosaurs in 4th grade? Geography in the 8th? Biology in the 9th? Geometry in the 10th? Literature in the 12th?

Or are you unwilling to call any of those excitements "intellectual"? Do you have to move mentally to your college years to find your first intellectual excitement?

And where did you find that? In physics? In calculus? In philosophy? In French literature?

Or was it in theology, or in chemistry, or in world history?

Or, if you studied pedagogy, did that first intellectual excitement occur when you examined developmental reading theory for the first time, and began to draw for yourself a portrait of how a child's mind first grapples with written symbols?

Wherever that experience was and however young or old you were, recall the characteristics of the event or events. What—exactly—intrigued you? How were the ideas delivered to your mind? What seeds were planted inside you then?

If the experience developed in a classroom, what made you actually look forward to the next meeting of the class? What made you reflect upon the class after it ended and you no longer "had" to think about it?

Pause now for just a moment, if you will. Look away from the page and remember that early eagerness to know more. Picture the people immersed with you in that endeavor: the teacher or professor, your classmates, perhaps your parents. Remember how you imagined yourself going forward with your life from that point, with your perspectives altered and your mind opened by new patterns and new paradigms.

Now think back again, but not as far (presumably) into the past.

Try to remember your LAST encounter with intellectual excitement.

Not the last time you *provided* intellectual excitement for your students (important though that certainly is), but the last time you yourself *experienced* the kind of intellectual excitement you were recalling just 30 seconds ago.

If you are in the same situation as that in which many teachers find themselves, your most recent experience of true intellectual excitement is not particularly recent. It is a more distant memory.

Think about that paradox. To teach well by the principles developed in ISM's studies and presented in this workbook, inspiring your students is a fundamental component in developing persistence, strong performance, high levels of satisfaction, and sustained enthusiasm in those students. In turn, renewing your "professional self" is a fundamental component in maintaining persistence, strong performance, high levels of satisfaction, and sustained enthusiasm in *yourself*.

Recall the following items from Chapters Two and Three of this workbook.

Professional Characteristic Seven: *I demonstrate believably high levels of enthusiasm for teaching/learning and for the content of my studies.*

Professional Characteristic Fourteen: *I pursue career-long professional development as a foremost priority.*

Professional Characteristic Fifteen: *I am knowledgeable of cutting-edge content and developmental theory.*

Professional Characteristic Sixteen: *I have mastered at least one pedagogical approach that is supported by reliable, contemporary research outcomes.*

Professional Characteristic Twenty-Seven: *I am practiced in communicating in-class experimentation-and-testing outcomes and findings to colleagues, within and beyond the school.*

Professional Characteristic Twenty-Eight: *I am practiced in routine (yet enthusiastic) participation in outside-the-school academic organizations whose work is supportive of, and pertinent to, my field(s).*

Consider these six Professional Characteristics in their totality. Think about the implied relationships among them. They bespeak enthusiasm for:

- teaching/learning;
- the content of your material;
- professional development as a foremost priority;
- cutting-edge theory;
- research-supported teaching methods;

– in-your-own-classroom experimentation;

– "cross-pollination" with colleagues both within and beyond your school; and

– participation in relevant-to-you academic organizations and associations.

We know the adage, "A rising tide lifts all boats." Certainly, you can "renew your professional self" as a solo activity, simply as a step in reinforcing in yourself the high levels of performance, satisfaction, and enthusiasm that we know to be associated with the strongest student and faculty cultures. But we also know that linking yourself to a colleague, or to several colleagues, or to your academic department, or to your lower/middle/upper-school division faculty, or to your whole-school faculty, or to academic organizations beyond your school—any or all of these steps—is likely to make your long-term self-renewal more certain and more gratifying.

This is why each of the self-rating scales in Chapters Two and Three took you beyond rating your current level to that of your three-year goal as well as to that of your faculty colleagues (in your own estimation). Working alone or with colleagues, set out to recapture something of the seminal enthusiasm that led you to this profession.

There is a sense in which this should become part of the "due diligence" of the vocation itself. It is simply not enough to coast forward in this career, having mastered the rudiments of teaching and having reached a level of intellectual and pedagogical competence.

Your students—and you—deserve much, much more.

Notes:

Community: Tests

Your adherence, or not, to the teaching approaches necessary to create and sustain a "predictable and supportive" environment often reveals itself clearly in your approach to test creation, test giving, and test scoring/grading. Three of the Professional Characteristics shown in Chapter Two are especially pertinent here. Because each of these characteristics is easily misunderstood or misinterpreted, the "Comment" for each is included.

Professional Characteristic Three: *I set clearly articulated standards for student academic performance.*

Comment: This is a statement not about your own scoring and grading system itself. It is about your ability and willingness to illuminate the nature of your academic expectations, i.e., *not* about explaining that 90–93 = A- and 94–97 = A and 98–100 = A+, but delineating (in age-appropriate fashion, of course) the subject-specific levels of mastery that you expect from your students. An illustration of this might entail providing students with examples (before an assignment) of submissions that you would grade as A, B, C, and so on, or involving your students in the development of the rubric.

Professional Characteristic Ten: *I create predictable tests (not to be confused either with "simple" tests or with "easy" tests). My students can rely on the test preparation that I offer them.*

Comment: This statement emphasizes the principle that tests of any sort should reveal each student's grasp of facts, concepts, and/or their applications in problem-solving contexts. It is *not* about their abilities either to guess what the teacher means, to deal with unexpected testing formats, or to retrieve material that was not cited in assignments or in the test-review process. One of the surest ways to reduce levels of student performance, satisfaction, and enthusiasm is to test students in ways that leave them consistently feeling "tricked." Students should feel, upon receiving their grade, that they had been told what testing format to expect, what material would be covered, and something about the teacher's expectations (see Professional Characteristic No. 3, "Comment"). While authentic assessments that require students to demonstrate learned skills in new contexts can be excellent learning tools, students should know ahead of time that they will be asked to do this (if the context itself is not known). They should have had plenty of low-stakes practice applying skills to new contexts prior to the graded assessment.

Professional Characteristic Eleven: *I provide fair, reliable, understandable grade/reward structures for my students. My students are led to understand why they receive the grades they receive—good or bad—and thereby to see how improvement, if they will seek it, might be possible.*

Comment: While the words "fair," "reliable," and "understandable" connote this Professional Characteristic's transparent relationship to "predictability," its relationship to "supportiveness" is even more critical. The simplest way to say this is that your feedback to your students on anything that is graded should leave them feeling *hopeful* that improvement might be possible. Your explicit comments—written or oral—on the steps needed to improve are considerably more important than the grade itself in this process. While the "improvement ball" always remains in your students' court, so to speak, the teacher's role must always include further instructions on the grip, the swing, the tactics, and the strategy. The least *and* the most academically gifted of your students must feel an unquestioning confidence that you expect them to get better, from the first day of school to the last.

Testing and grading, on the one hand, and teaching and learning, on the other, sometimes dovetail so thoroughly that it is hard to envision where one ends and the other begins. Examples come readily to mind.

Picture a skillfully taught third-year foreign language class. In such a setting, testing and teaching often become indistinguishable as the teacher assists, cajoles, prods, hints, and shares in the daily translation process, all the while making judgments about both the students' progress toward excellence and about the quality and effectiveness of his/her own instructional approach.

Now imagine a third-grade reading session conducted by a skilled veteran. Once more, testing and teaching become indistinguishable from each other, as the teacher simultaneously assists the students, makes judgments about the students, and makes judgments about the effectiveness of his own instructional process.

These have in common simultaneous *helping and judging activities* by a skilled teacher.

Now return to the kind of scenario we tend to imagine more commonly when the subject is testing and grading. Imagine a thoroughly traditional, upper-school mathematics class. No group projects are underway; no mathematical concepts are being "discovered" via some version of an inquiry method. The teacher is straightforwardly preparing the class for the mid-grading-period exam one week from today. The teacher's goal is to spend at least one minute in explicit, in-class test preparation for every two minutes of examination time.

Since this exam will last an hour, the teacher will spend at least 30 minutes in class describing the test in detail. She will provide sample questions, give sample answers to the questions, and demonstrate the exact steps she plans to use in grading—thereby giving a sample scoring procedure for the sample answers to the sample questions.

Further, during the weeklong period between this session and the exam itself, this traditional-method teacher will blur the line between "teaching" and "testing" in much the same way as did the foreign language teacher mentioned previously. Entirely apart from the time spent in *explicit* test preparation, she will repeatedly quiz the students orally on the concepts and procedures to be featured on the exam. By so doing, she will make judgments both about the students' individual progress and about her own effectiveness in moving them toward the examination's goals.

It is this continual process of providing positive and negative reinforcement, day after day, hour after hour, minute after minute, which establishes clear connections in students' minds between what they do and the results of what they do. As emphasized earlier in this workbook, it is this clarity of cause/effect connection in students' minds that is associated with the persistence, performance, satisfaction, and enthusiasm that most teachers hope to develop—and to develop *deliberately*—in their students.

At least as important, though, this continual attention to the blending of teaching and testing provides *the teacher* with evidence of cause-effect connection, which is just as critical to her or him as to the students. Where this connection is reinforced daily, the teacher, too, is more likely to maintain high levels of *instructional* persistence, performance, and personal/ professional satisfaction and enthusiasm.

In environments wherein learned optimism is generated consistently by the faculty and in which, consequently, the sense of community is strong, even the most unsuccessful students tend to declare confidently that teachers makes clear to them what they should do to succeed. They also declare themselves secure in their certainty that their teachers are on their side, and declare that, once they decide to "get in gear," everything will be fine. (They may, at the same time, acknowledge the possibility that they will never choose to "get in gear.")

Conversely, in environments in which learned helplessness is generated consistently by the faculty and in which, consequently, the sense of community is weak, the most successful of students will assert that they succeed *despite* the faculty—in Angela Duckworth's terms, they succeed only as a result of their "gritty determination." They are also certain beyond question that their success or failure is of interest to their teachers *only* in the sense that, when they graduate and move to the next level of schooling, their teachers will take interest and pride in their acceptance into a strong institution.

This last is not necessarily a terrible state of affairs. But it is nonetheless regrettable. It is regrettable in that both teachers and students will have performed at levels well below their individual capacities, will have experienced satisfaction levels well below those they might have known, and will have felt far less enthusiasm for their school experience than that which was within their collective reach.

Notes:

Community: Responsibility

ISM's studies over a period of two decades and ISM's corporate experience over a period approaching four decades have pointed to a set of relationships between teachers and students—students of any age—that are psychologically and emotionally healthy. In schools in which student performance, satisfaction, and enthusiasm are strong, teachers have tended to have high academic expectations of their students, yes. But they have also tended to display conspicuously high levels of supportiveness for their students' efforts.

Hand-in-hand with that teacher-supportiveness goes an excitement about, a commitment to, and an immersion in students' academic and cocurricular progress that appears to relegate "control"—for its own sake—to the back row. These teachers, paradoxically enough, are just too busy with their basic professional reasons-for-being to invest huge amounts of time and energy in behavioral minutiae.

They are so prepared, so organized, so focused, so excited about what they are teaching—and so committed to getting their students "on task" while in class—they just cannot take the view that every behavioral irregularity must be confronted and beaten down. They can, in short, be "taken advantage of" in small ways without feeling a great deal of concern about that fact.

There tends to be a grudging good-naturedness about these teachers' expectations of their students' behaviors. There tends to be a willingness to say, at least implicitly, "If you work as hard as I expect, I will give you a *little* leeway behaviorally, especially in your interactions with your peers."

This should not be taken as an indication that a *laissez-faire* approach to classroom behavior control is being recommended. The emphasis here is, rather, on the rationality and defensibleness of your behavioral expectations, and the good-naturedness with which you apply those expectations.

Recall the language of Professional Characteristic Four in Chapter Two of this workbook. And note especially the "Comment" paragraph.

Professional Characteristic Four: *I set reasonable, defensible standards for student behavior.*

Comment: This is a statement not about schoolwide rules and regulations, but about the behavioral expectations you develop for students in your own classroom. The statement implies that your behavioral expectations should be spelled out—possibly in writing and posted in your classroom—and, beyond that, should be explained in ways that are intelligible to your students. (It is worth remembering that "bad laws make hard cases." Your standards for student behavior in your classroom should relate to the school mission and should be viewed by students as *reasonable* applications of that mission.) As a community-building opportunity at the beginning of the year, consider involving your students in the development of classroom rules, etiquette, and expectations.

Picture a middle-school hallway between classes. Controlled chaos reigns. Teachers who will demand courteously, two minutes from now, that their students sit down promptly and immediately prepare their desks for *work*, now comfortably watch students being kid-like, intervening only when safety or decibel issues require.

This benign tolerance for hallway goofiness changes into a focused expectation—convertible in a heartbeat to a courteous demand, if necessary—that every student's attention is snapped onto the teacher herself/himself for start-of-academic-business. This takes sustained, daily practice on the part of both teachers and students, as does everything that you wish to become habitual in yourself and your students.

The alternatives to "context-determined behavioral expectations" do not work. If the hallway looseness continues into the classroom's academic environment, performance suffers. If lock-step behavior is required in the middle-school hallway, a sense of oppression will prevail. The results of *either* of these are predictable: a weak sense of community, little success in teaching the meaning of responsibility and adult-like behavior, and plenty of student/teacher tension.

Student performance—for any age/grade level—flourishes when students are treated by their teachers in ways that:

(a) enhance their self-perceived worth;

(b) demonstrate their teachers' high expectations (including expectations for an age-appropriate version of "adult-like behavior"); and

(c) communicate the idea that their teachers are "on their side" and "desire their success" (and yet demand focused commitment to the academic task at hand).

Review and Conclusion

Chapter Two—prior to its display of the 13 top-tier professional characteristics—noted the following. Take a moment to review, keeping in mind that there is no single "correct" way to use the material in this workbook. Here are a few of your choices.

- Work through the material as an individual, using the workbook-like pages to score yourself, to reach decisions about changes in your own approach that you might wish to attempt, and to set professional development goals for yourself.

- Do the same in cooperation with one or more of your peers, meeting periodically to discuss these ideas, to initiate individual or small-group (pedagogical) trials—a form of "action research"—and to compare notes week-by-week and month-by-month.

- Involve your administrator(s) to:

    (a) perform a whole-faculty self-scoring on the ISM School Culture Matrix Instrument and Scoring Chart (Appendix A);

    (b) discuss the outcomes vis-à-vis the ISM School Culture Matrix (shown previously in Chapter One);

    (c) administer the Student Experience Profile II (Appendix B);

    (d) administer the Faculty Culture Profile II (Appendix C);

    (e) incorporate the Characteristics of Professional Excellence II (Chapters 2–3, pp. 103–110) into your approach to faculty evaluation; and/or

    (f) in other creative ways, integrate your own work in this book with the in-parallel work of your colleagues, with the long-term goal of establishing and maintaining your faculty culture's position in the upper-right quadrant of the ISM School Culture Matrix.

You are now in better position to understand those three bullet points—and their implications—than when you first read them in Chapter Two. And so you have a sense of how quickly you can multiply the whole-school effects of implementation of these professional characteristics when that implementation rises above the single-teacher level to the faculty peer-group level (e.g., grade level, department level) to the divisional level to the whole-faculty level. And it is at these latter levels—the divisional level and the whole-faculty level—that it becomes meaningful to speak of *the faculty culture*. At those levels, your school's students, and you, begin to experience those qualities you read in the upper-right quadrant of the ISM School Culture Matrix.

And there, operating within a fully "predictable and supportive" environment, your school's students—all of them—will be afforded the finest possible conditions under which to maximize their performance, satisfaction, and enthusiasm, one student at a time. And the same will be true of their teachers.

ISM School Culture Matrix Instrument, Scoring Instructions, and Scoring Chart

The questions in this faculty culture survey are based on ISM's findings in the Student Experience Study (SES), which indicated primary predictors of student performance, satisfaction, and enthusiasm. As opposed to a faculty satisfaction survey, ISM's focus in this survey is on the overall climate or culture of the school—as opposed to a focus on the individual.

Each question begins with the phrase, **"I and my colleagues..."** Though you cannot speak with complete accuracy for your colleagues, what interests us for the purpose of this survey is your perspective on the issues and *your impressions* of your colleagues' perspectives on the issues.

ISM School Culture Matrix Instrument

Circle only one number for each item. Consider in your responses only the three most recent months unless otherwise instructed.

1. I and my colleagues understand exactly how we are evaluated.

1	2	3	4	5	6	7	8	9
(Not true at all)								*(Exactly True)*

2. I and my colleagues view our evaluation procedures as consistent (i.e., predictable).

1	2	3	4	5	6	7	8	9
(Not true at all)								*(Exactly True)*

3. I and my colleagues view our evaluation procedures as constructive (i.e., helpful).

1	2	3	4	5	6	7	8	9
(Not true at all)								*(Exactly True)*

4. I and my colleagues view our faculty culture as appropriately supportive (as evidenced by collegial interaction).

1	2	3	4	5	6	7	8	9
(Not true at all)								*(Exactly True)*

5. _I and my colleagues view our school's administrative culture (i.e., the collective attitude of all our administrative staff members, including those in the business office, development office, admission office, and so on) as appropriately supportive of the faculty, i.e., wishing our success and striving to support us in our efforts._

| 1 | 2 | 3 | 4 | 5 | 6 | 7 | 8 | 9 |

(Not true at all)   _(Exactly True)_

6. _I and my colleagues find that the administrator(s) who supervises and/or evaluates us is highly supportive of us, i.e., hopes for our success and is focused on our growth and renewal as professionals._

| 1 | 2 | 3 | 4 | 5 | 6 | 7 | 8 | 9 |

(Not true at all)   _(Exactly True)_

7. _I and my colleagues agree that the administrator(s) who supervises and/or evaluates us provides us with accurate positive reinforcement and/or negative reinforcement regarding our performance as faculty members._

| 1 | 2 | 3 | 4 | 5 | 6 | 7 | 8 | 9 |

(Not true at all)   _(Exactly True)_

8. _I and my colleagues agree that the administrator(s) who supervises and/or evaluates us demonstrates consistent responses on a daily basis. We find that we know what to expect from her/him in all situations._

| 1 | 2 | 3 | 4 | 5 | 6 | 7 | 8 | 9 |

(Not true at all)   _(Exactly True)_

9. _I and my colleagues agree that the administrator(s) who supervises us and/or evaluates us provides clarity of expectations._

| 1 | 2 | 3 | 4 | 5 | 6 | 7 | 8 | 9 |

(Not true at all)   _(Exactly True)_

10. I and my colleagues agree that the administrator(s) who supervises us and/or evaluates us is eager to assist us in meeting those expectations.

1	*2*	*3*	*4*	*5*	*6*	*7*	*8*	*9*

(Not true at all)   *(Exactly True)*

Scoring Instructions

A. Determine your faculty's (or your faculty unit's) mean score for each of the ten items.

B. Average the mean scores for items 3, 4, 5, 6, and 10.

C. Go to the ISM School Culture Matrix Scoring Chart, and on the horizontal "supportiveness" axis, circle the nearest whole number to reflect your average/mean.

D. Average the mean scores for items 1, 2, 7, 8, and 9.

E. Go to the ISM School Culture Matrix Scoring Chart, and on the vertical "predictability" axis, circle the nearest whole number to reflect your average/mean.

F. At the intersection of the vertical and horizontal axis scores, place a star to indicate your faculty's self-placement on the ISM School Culture Matrix Scoring Chart. Then make reference to the ISM School Culture Matrix itself (see Chapter One), where you will find lists of the general characteristics to be expected in each of the quadrants.

Comment: Although the quadrant-placement concept is derived from decades of ISM research into faculty and student cultures, the quadrant-placement scoring system itself is not a research outcome. Use your quadrant-placement outcomes to extend the faculty-culture conversation with your teachers. Emphasize the statistical relationship between faculty culture characteristics and student culture characteristics and, thus, with student performance, satisfaction, and enthusiasm.

Scoring Chart

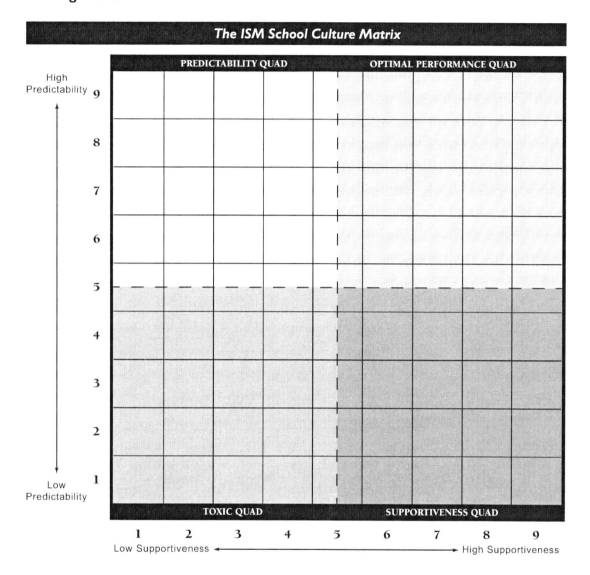

The ISM School Culture Matrix

PREDICTABILITY QUAD   OPTIMAL PERFORMANCE QUAD

High Predictability 9

8

7

6

5

4

3

2

Low Predictability 1

TOXIC QUAD   SUPPORTIVENESS QUAD

1   2   3   4   5   6   7   8   9

Low Supportiveness ◄   ► High Supportiveness

ISM Student Experience Profile II

Your school's results from the ISM Student Experience Profile II should, ISM suggests, serve as one basis for ongoing professional-development-focused conversations with individual teachers and, as well, with whole-faculty groups and sub-groups. (Note: this instrument was developed within grade 5–12 contexts, and is designed for use by students in those grade levels, inclusive.)

Circle only one number for each item. Consider only the most recent grading period in your responses.

1. I have very much looked forward to coming to school every day of this grading period.

1	2	3	4	5	6	7	8	9

Not true of me at all)   *Exactly true of me*

2. I have not seen or heard of unkind behavior—of anybody being "picked on" in any way at all—anywhere in our school during this grading period.

1	2	3	4	5	6	7	8	9

Absolutely no unkind behavior   *Unkind behavior every day*

3. I find that I am proud of my school and proud to be part of such a school.

1	2	3	4	5	6	7	8	9

Not true of me at all   *Exactly true of me*

*4. It has been obvious to me that my teachers **really** want me to do well—in school and out of school.*

1	2	3	4	5	6	7	8	9

Not accurate at all   *Fully accurate*

5. My teachers have worked every day at helping me become a better, more virtuous person, regardless of the subject they are teaching (math, science, English, history, etc.).

| 1 | 2 | 3 | 4 | 5 | 6 | 7 | 8 | 9 |

Not accurate at all   Fully accurate

6. I have been very excited about what I've been studying this grading period (the course material itself, not the teaching of the material).

| 1 | 2 | 3 | 4 | 5 | 6 | 7 | 8 | 9 |

No, zero excitement   Yes, tremendous excitement

7. I'm so satisfied with my school, I'd certainly want to come here, if my family and I could choose again.

| 1 | 2 | 3 | 4 | 5 | 6 | 7 | 8 | 9 |

No, absolutely not   Yes, certainly

8. Our tests this grading period have covered exactly what my teachers said they would cover.

| 1 | 2 | 3 | 4 | 5 | 6 | 7 | 8 | 9 |

No, our teachers always tried to trick us   Yes, our tests covered exactly what we were told to study

9. All the grades I received during this grading period—big tests, quizzes, papers, etc.—were exactly the grades I think I actually earned—no higher or lower.

| 1 | 2 | 3 | 4 | 5 | 6 | 7 | 8 | 9 |

Never the correct grade   Always the correct grade

10. I have been completely satisfied with our rules (including the dress code).

| 1 | 2 | 3 | 4 | 5 | 6 | 7 | 8 | 9 |

Terrible, stupid rules   Perfectly appropriate rules

11. *Our teachers have enforced our rules (including the dress code) justly, fairly, consistently.*

1	2	3	4	5	6	7	8	9

Unfair or no enforcement   *Fair, just enforcement*

12. *I have known exactly what to expect from my teachers every day; I have known just how they will react to anything we say or do.*

1	2	3	4	5	6	7	8	9

Teachers moody and unpredictable   *Teachers perfectly consistent every day*

To score the Student Experience Profile II so as to make outcomes comparable to this study's outcomes (See Appendix E, Table I: Pearson Product-Moment Correlations/Significance Levels by Grading Period; Means for Each Scale by Grading Period: GPA; P&S; Satisfaction; Enthusiasm), break each student's scores into the three scales: Predictability and Support scale: items 2, 4, 5, 8, 9, 11, 12 (item 2 reverse scored); Satisfaction scale: items 1, 7, 10; Enthusiasm scale: items 1, 3, 6. (Item 1 is double-scored.) Thus, for a given student, the P/S scale's maximum score is 63 (9 x 7 items); the Satisfaction and Enthusiasm scales' maximum scores are 27 each (9 x 3 items).

Notes:

ISM Faculty Culture Profile II

The ISM Faculty Culture Profile II differs from ISM's earlier iterations of the profile in that the revised version's Part A ties explicitly to the ISM Student Experience Profile II. This faculty culture instrument links strongly, then, to the ISM findings in the Student Experience Study regarding student performance, student satisfaction, and student enthusiasm. Your own school's outcomes from the two instruments may profitably be considered companion pieces in your ongoing efforts to monitor the extent to which "predictability and support" conditions are present, and how strongly so, within your teaching/learning environment. (ISM continues to recommend that the Faculty Culture Profile II be given in fall, winter and spring, with an Evaluation Design Team of exemplary teachers administering the instrument and assisting faculty leaders/administrators in the interpretation of the outcomes, item-by-item.)

The questions in this faculty culture survey are based on ISM's findings in the Student Experience Study (SES), which indicated primary predictors of student performance, satisfaction, and enthusiasm. As opposed to a faculty satisfaction survey, ISM's focus in this survey is on the overall climate or culture of the school—as opposed to a focus on the individual.

Each question begins with the phrase, **"I and my colleagues…"** Though you cannot speak with complete accuracy for your colleagues, what interests us for the purpose of this survey is your perspective on the issues and *your impressions* of your colleagues' perspectives on the issues.

Part A: Faculty culture items related to the Student Experience Profile II

Circle only one number for each item.

Consider only the most recent grading period in your responses unless otherwise directed.

1. I and my colleagues find ways to make it obvious to all students that we wish them success every day, both in school and outside of school.

1	2	3	4	5	6	7	8	9

Not true of us at all   Exactly true of us

2. I and my colleagues find ways to make it obvious to all students that we want them to become better, more virtuous people (in ways consistent with our school's stated purposes and projected outcomes for our graduates).

1	2	3	4	5	6	7	8	9

Not true of us at all   Exactly true of us

3. I and my colleagues set clearly articulated standards for student academic performance.

| 1 | 2 | 3 | 4 | 5 | 6 | 7 | 8 | 9 |

Not true of us at all   Exactly true of us

4. I and my colleagues set reasonable, defensible standards for student behavior.

| 1 | 2 | 3 | 4 | 5 | 6 | 7 | 8 | 9 |

Not true of us at all   Exactly true of us

5. I and my colleagues are continually alert to displays of unkindness among students in my efforts to ensure a safe physical and emotional environment

| 1 | 2 | 3 | 4 | 5 | 6 | 7 | 8 | 9 |

Not true of us at all   Exactly true of us

6. In confrontations with students, I and my colleagues conduct ourselves in ways that leave students' dignity intact regardless of the nature of the issue or infraction.

1   2   3   4   5   6   7   8   9

Not true of us at all   Exactly true of us

7. I and my colleagues individually and collectively demonstrate believably high levels of enthusiasm for teaching/ learning and for the content of our studies.

| 1 | 2 | 3 | 4 | 5 | 6 | 7 | 8 | 9 |

Not true of us at all   Exactly true of us

8. I and my colleagues demonstrate through words and actions a genuine, believable commitment to the school, its purposes, its leadership, and each other.

| 1 | 2 | 3 | 4 | 5 | 6 | 7 | 8 | 9 |

Not true of us at all   Exactly true of us

9. I and my colleagues are glad to arrive at school and to see our students each day.

1	2	3	4	5	6	7	8	9

Not true of us at all   Exactly true of us

10. I and my colleagues create predictable tests (not to be confused either with "simple" tests or with "easy" tests). Our students can rely on the test preparation we offer them.

1	2	3	4	5	6	7	8	9

Not true of us at all   Exactly true of us

11. I and my colleagues provide fair, reliable, understandable grade/reward structures for our students. Our students are led to understand why they receive the grades they receive—good or bad—and thereby to see how improvement, if they will seek it, might be possible.

1	2	3	4	5	6	7	8	9

Not true of us at all   Exactly true of us

12. I and my colleagues enforce our rules, including the dress code, justly, fairly, consistently.

1	2	3	4	5	6	7	8	9

Not true of us at all   Exactly true of us

13. I and my colleagues are able to present ourselves each day in ways that will be seen by our students as consistent and reliable (i.e., unaffected by outside-of-school problems).

1	2	3	4	5	6	7	8	9

Not true of us at all   Exactly true of us

Part B: Selected faculty culture items related to the original ISM study of students and teachers, and found in the Faculty Culture Profile I

14. *I and my colleagues individually and collectively pursue career-long professional development as a foremost priority.*

1	2	3	4	5	6	7	8	9

Not true of us at all   Exactly true of us

15. *I and my colleagues have mastered at least one pedagogical approach—not necessarily the same one for all of us—that is supported by reliable, contemporary research outcomes.*

1	2	3	4	5	6	7	8	9

Not true of us at all   Exactly true of us

16. *When I and my colleagues are in casual conversations with each other, those conversations tend to be constructive, upbeat, and professional.*

1	2	3	4	5	6	7	8	9

Not true of us at all   Exactly true of us

17. *I and my colleagues have great respect for our division and/or school administrators.*

1	2	3	4	5	6	7	8	9

Not true of us at all   Exactly true of us

18. *I and my colleagues find that our division and/or school administrators are highly supportive of our division's and/or school's faculty.*

1	2	3	4	5	6	7	8	9

Not true of us at all   Exactly true of us

19. *I and my colleagues find that our division and/or school administrators are highly supportive of our division's and/or school's students.*

| 1 | 2 | 3 | 4 | 5 | 6 | 7 | 8 | 9 |

Not true of us at all   *Exactly true of us*

20. *I and my colleagues find that our division and/or school administrators are highly supportive of our division's and/or school's parents.*

| 1 | 2 | 3 | 4 | 5 | 6 | 7 | 8 | 9 |

Not true of us at all   *Exactly true of us*

To score the Faculty Culture Profile II using the method that will conform to appropriate self-scoring on the ISM Stability Marker pertaining to the quality of the faculty culture, use the following method. On any item on which 75% or more of the faculty members score at the top third of the response scale (i.e., 75% or more of the faculty circling the 7, 8, or 9), award one point. After determining the total (a number between 0 and 20, since there are 20 items), multiply that number by 0.3, thus converting the outcome to the six-point scale required by that item in the ISM Stability Markers.

Notes:

ISM's Original Twenty Principles for Teaching Excellence

The Foundation: Principles One Through Ten

1. I am academically *authoritative*—broadly and thoroughly knowledgeable—in my fields of expertise. (This includes, for elementary teachers, developmental reading theory, developmental mathematics theory, developmental psychomotor theory, and other pertinent theoretical-research areas.)

2. I am *current* in my fields of academic expertise. (This includes, for elementary teachers, those areas shown in Principle One. "Current" assumes *formal study within the last 36 months*, together with regular reviews of cutting-edge journals in all relevant disciplines.)

3. I hold high (but not uniform) expectations of *all* of my students.

4. I set high (but not uniform), overtly and *repeatedly articulated* standards for *all* of my students.

5. In my classes, student "time-on-task" (students engaged in active, not passive, learning, testing, and/or drill activities) is 50% of total class time or higher, *regardless of discipline, grade level, or age.*

6. I allocate for explicit test preparation of my students at least one minute of class test-preparation time for every two minutes of testing time.

7. I view test preparation as an integral part of the teaching process and consciously "teach to the test."

8. My approach to grading includes subjectivity (even in scoring "objective" tests) and attention to psychological reinforcement principles.

9. My students—even those exhibiting the "worst" behaviors—would agree that my approach to classroom behavior control is both fair and humane.

10. My approach to classroom behavior control is *consistent, rigorous, includes confrontations as needed,* and is based upon the principle of "individual equity," as distinct from principles of "justice and fairness." *It is consistent with my instructional mission and with "community building"* in my classroom. Students, having been confronted by me, still *have their dignity intact* and remain clear that I am "on their side" and "desire their success."

The Refinements: Principles 11 Through 20

11. Regardless of age/grade levels of students, I endeavor to be professionally/emotionally involved with my students outside of class (for example, via *enthusiastic* arranging and supervising of appropriate field trips, *vigorous* club sponsorship, or, in middle and upper schools, through passionate drama production supervision or *"grown-up," philosophically defensible, role-model-appropriate* coaching of sports teams—all tailored thoughtfully to the developmental levels of the children or young adults involved).

12. Aside from my direct involvement (Principle Eleven), I display an overt, conspicuous interest in my students' outside-of-class lives, *without crossing the psychological barrier* of privacy invasion.

13. My teaching approach includes giving "responsibility" and "adult-like roles" to my students, regardless of their developmental age, through such vehicles as choice-within-structure ("complete these two tasks by eleven o'clock; you may decide the order in which you will work on them"), within-class leadership development tactics ("you coordinate the work of these two small groups"), and/or extra-class leadership development tactics ("you four make a plan for the March field trip and submit it for whole-class consideration by next Friday").

14. My goals for the students and my standards for the students' performance are overtly "taught" by me in a planned progression throughout the school year.

15. My approach is to treat students as individuals within common frames of reference (for example, giving a "B" to Maria, who normally writes an error-free essay but this time made five mistakes, and a similar grade to Rosa, who normally writes miserable essays but this time made a "mere" 10 errors) rather than treating them "all alike."

16. Regardless of the "subject" I am teaching at a given moment, I endeavor to lead my students' "awareness" beyond the immediacy of the self and toward "the community" (broadly conceived as peers, the totality of the school, the neighborhoods represented in the classroom, the town, city, state, nation, world), and I do so systematically in my content decisions (for example, in selection of word problems in mathematics, in applications for chemistry solutions, in bulletin-board materials for first-graders).

17. When I encounter and/or develop individual or group student *excellence* ("excellence" relative to that student's or those students' capabilities and points of departure), I recognize—that is, psychologically reinforce—that excellence both privately and publicly.

18. When I encounter and/or develop individual or group student *effort* which is noteworthy ("effort" relative to that student's or those students' capabilities and points of departure), I recognize—that is, psychologically reinforce—that effort both privately and publicly.

19. I understand psychological *reinforcement principles* in depth.

20. Implementation of psychological *reinforcement principles* is a regular, minute-by-minute component of my approach to teaching.

The Replication Project: Detail

Eight private-independent schools representing a range of "types" (single-sex/coed, religious/secular, boarding/day, with/without grades 9–12) agreed to participate in a year-long partial replication of the original ISM International Model Schools Project, which had in the mid-1990s identified the critical variables associated with student performance, student satisfaction, and student enthusiasm. Those paired variables, termed "predictability and support" by ISM, have provided a flexible pedagogical framework within which whole faculties and/or individual teachers, using any teaching method whatever, could, by observing the predictability/support principles, enhance the likelihood that students would perform better and experience strengthened satisfaction from, and enthusiasm for, their school experiences.

As noted previously in this chapter, "predictability and support" have been (and continue to be) defined by ISM as a school environment in which students find that:

- the rule/reward structure is strong, but intelligible and fair from the student perspective;

- faculty/administration/coaching responses are consistent, fair, and accurate from the student perspective, in regard to what is positively or negatively reinforced (both academically and behaviorally); and,

- the faculty, administration, and coaching staffs appear to the students genuinely to desire their (the students') success and work to elicit that success, but nonetheless provide accurate—not inflated—reinforcement (as implied by the first two items in this list).

Thirteen to sixteen grade 5–11 students at each of the eight schools, representing a broad achievement range at each school, were interviewed by ISM Consultant/data collectors at the end of each grading period, and copies of their report cards were submitted to ISM (signed parental permission forms having been collected at the start). Pearson Product-Moment correlation outcomes supported the original (1990s) findings: Predictability/support principles—whether used purposefully or "accidentally" *(i.e., as a byproduct of a particular teaching approach or as a teacher-specific idiosyncrasy)* in classrooms, in hallways, on playing fields, in administrative offices—correlated significantly with student performance, satisfaction, and enthusiasm.

ISM concludes afresh that those who lead faculties should:

- seek to build faculty cultures in which predictability/support principles predominate, *regardless of the prevailing pedagogical style, if any, imbedded in the existing faculty culture;* and

- evaluate individual teachers, at least in part, on the basis of their adherence to predictability/support principles, using an evaluation tool that teachers themselves find predictable and supportive.

ISM calls particular attention to the certainty that instructional delivery systems will emphasize technology at ever-increasing levels throughout the 21st century. Predictability and support principles can provide a conceptual framework that is flexible yet reliable, permitting faculties and their leaders to approach a technology-dominated future appropriately equipped to navigate difficult teaching/learning routes with confidence.

Method

Eight schools were engaged in early fall of the 2010–11 school year. The schools collectively provided the study with single-sex and coed contexts: with PK–5, PK–8, PK–12, 7–12, and 9–12 grade configurations; with religiously affiliated and secular missions; and with day and boarding environments. At each school, 13–16 students were invited to participate. Students were selected by school administrators to conform to ISM's requirements: students from each academic quartile; boys and girls equally (except in the three single-sex schools); no students likely to be intimidated by interviewers from outside the school community (i.e., by ISM personnel). Students were interviewed in pairs, near the end of each grading period.

ISM developed an interview instrument designed to measure:

- student perception of "predictability and support" in the environment,
- student satisfaction, and
- student enthusiasm.

These were the three most critical findings—in their relationship to student performance and to each other—from the earlier six-year 1990s ISM project.

Findings, in tabular form, are shown following (see page 99 fo pairings).

Table I: Pearson Product-Moment Correlations/Significance Levels by Grading Period; Means for Each Scale by Grading Period (GPA, P/S, Satisfaction, Enthusiasm)			
	Fall	**Winter**	**Spring**
Total Students	N=121	N=108	N=116
Pairing 1	r = .119/.1	r = .225/.01	r = .254/.01
Pairing 2	r = .523/.001	r = .699/.001	r = .748/.001
Pairing 3	r = .513/.001	r = .670/.001	r = .681/.001
Pairing 4	r = - .044/NS	r = .075/NS	r = .210/.1
Pairing 5	r = - .096/NS	r = .052/NS	r = .045/NS
Cumulative GPAs	3.326	3.243	3.267
Predictability/support	52.30	48.56	47.91
Satisfaction	20.52	18.60	18.28
Enthusiasm	19.96	18.44	18.17

Note 1: All correlation significance tests were directional.
Note 2: GPAs on 4.0 scale; predictability/support on 63-point scale; both satisfaction and enthusiasm on 27-point scales; GPAs calculated by ISM based only upon grades in English, math, science, social studies/history, theology or other faith-specific components of religious-mission-focused curricula, and world languages.

Findings and Comments on Findings

Pearson Product-Moment correlations were administered for each grading period, using the following five pairings.

1. Student-perceived "predictability and support" by student performance

2. Student-perceived "predictability and support" by student-reported satisfaction

3. Student-perceived "predictability and support" by student-reported enthusiasm

4. Student performance by student-reported satisfaction

5. Student performance by student-reported enthusiasm

Pairings 1, 2, and 3 reached statistical significance in each of the three grading periods (fall, winter, and spring) utilized in the study. (See Table 1 for detail.)

Pairing 4 failed to reach statistical significance in the fall and winter grading periods, but did reach statistical significance in the spring. (See Table 1 for detail.)

Pairing 5 failed to reach statistical significance in any of the grading periods utilized in the study. (See Table 1 for detail.)

Additionally, means were calculated at the end of each grading period for each of the four scales: GPAs, predictability/support, satisfaction, and enthusiasm. Note that, *while GPAs were highest in the fall, lowest in winter, and recovered somewhat in spring, mean scores on predictability/support, satisfaction, and enthusiasm declined throughout the year.*

Recommendations

1. Faculty leaders—School Heads, Division Heads, Deans of Faculty, Department Chairs, Grade-Level Coordinators, Evaluation Design Teams of teachers—should take action on the ramifications of this study's confirmation of ISM's original (1990s) findings: The apparent likelihood that *any pedagogical approach whatsoever can prove efficacious, provided it is delivered with conviction and enthusiasm and in a manner likely to promote student-perceived predictability and supportiveness in the learning environment.* Those ramifications plausibly extend to at least the following areas: student academic distinction; student-culture esprit de corps; student retention; student recruitment (via positive word of mouth); parent satisfaction (via their children's positive word of mouth); faculty satisfaction; faculty- culture esprit de corps; and faculty retention.

2. Academic administrators should focus equally on career-long, student performance-satisfaction-and-enthusiasm-based interaction with *individual teachers,* on the one hand, and on student performance-satisfaction-and-enthusiasm-based *faculty-culture development,* on the other. The former includes high-performance expectations of individual teachers (with real consequences both for success and failure). The latter includes regular monitoring of the faculty culture and a "homegrown" approach to career-long faculty professional development for all teachers, both of these coupled with a consistent focus on "cross-pollination" between and among individual teachers.

3. Faculty leaders in various roles should consider using the following ISM instruments/publications as the basis for student-culture monitoring, analysis, and strengthening; for individual teacher career-long evaluation and support; *and* for whole-faculty-culture

monitoring, analysis, and strengthening (a) the Student Experience Profile II (see Appendix B of this book); (b) the Faculty Culture Profile II (see Appendix C of this book); (c) the Characteristics of Professional Excellence II, Parts A & B (see Appendix F of this book); and (d) ISM's book *Comprehensive Faculty Development* (2013).

The Mission Application Plan: A Framework for Use in Your Teacher Evaluation System

ISM's comprehensive approach to private-independent school personnel evaluation may be studied in the aptly named ISM book, *Comprehensive Faculty Development*. While the pages following in Appendix F are not designed to substitute for that comprehensive system/document, they do offer a convenient framework within which the 35 Professional Characteristics (Chapters Two and Three of this workbook) may be applied in your teacher evaluation system. We call this framework the Mission Application Plan (MAP).

- **Section One: Mission:** Record in this section your school's mission statement, and compose your own personal/professional mission statement; compare the two.

- **Section Two: Characteristics of Professional Excellence II:** Here you will find the same list of 35 professional characteristics that were shown and discussed in Chapters Two and Three of this workbook. Rate yourself on each, then meet with your faculty supervisor to discuss which of these may serve as your focal point(s) concerning evaluation and professional development for the upcoming school year.

- **Section Three: Objectives:** Here list your (preferably two) major evaluation and professional development objectives for the year.

- **Section Four: Route Descriptions:** Here list the steps you anticipate taking in order to move forward on your objectives.

- **Section Five: Criteria for Excellence:** Here record anticipated outcomes—products, processes, assessment points—of your work for the year.

SECTION ONE: Mission

School Mission Statement

Quote your school's mission statement and circle, highlight, or underscore core words and/or value phrases, OR simply select one or more words and/or phrases from your school's mission statement on which your will focus this year.

_____

_____

_____

_____

_____

_____

Personal/Professional Mission Statement

Compose your own personal/professional mission statement. Circle, highlight, or underscore words and/or phrases that have significant meaning for you. Be sure that your statement implies the answer to this question: "Other than needing to make a living, why this, now, with my life?"

_____

_____

_____

_____

_____

_____

SECTION TWO: Characteristics of Professional Excellence II

The CPE II can have a variety of uses, including as an ingredient in any school's approach to faculty evaluation and professional development. In that context, individual teachers conduct a self-evaluation, rating themselves on all or portions of the CPE II. At the same time, each teacher's supervising administrator rates each teacher in preparation for a conference in which teacher and supervisor compare ratings, focusing equally on items on which the two agree, partially agree, and fully disagree. In the latter case, the item(s) on which disagreement is pronounced (when the teacher's self-rating is substantially higher than the supervisor's rating of that teacher) usually becomes a focal point in that teacher's professional development program for the upcoming year. In the context of teacher evaluation, improvement may be required as a condition for continued employment. The value of using the CPE II: Part A in this context is the statistical connection among the CPE II: Part A items, the Faculty Culture Profile: Part A items, and the Student Experience Profile items. Thus, as a given teacher focuses on a particular item for improvement, she or he is simultaneously focusing on an item that has a statistical relationship to student performance, satisfaction, and enthusiasm.

ISM's comprehensive approach to faculty evaluation and development can be studied in the book *Comprehensive Faculty Development: A Guide to Attract, Retain, Develop, Reward, and Inspire*, published by ISM in 2013. The CPE II may be used within the context of CFD, or, indeed, within the context of any other approach to faculty evaluation and development.

ISM Characteristics of Professional Excellence II: Parts A & B and Individual Teacher (Self-)Rating Scales

The ISM Characteristics of Professional Excellence II (CPE II) is divided into two parts: Part A, items derived from the ISM Student Experience Study (these items identical to those in the Faculty Culture Profile II: Part A except for details of the items' wording); and Part B, items designed for broad administrative use in faculty hiring/dismissal, faculty evaluation, and the development of more general criteria for overall faculty excellence.

Part A

Circle only one number for each item.

1. *I find ways to make it obvious to all students that I wish them success every day, both in school and outside of school.*

1	2	3	4	5	6	7	8	9
Not true of me at all								Exactly true of me

2. *I find ways to make it obvious to all students that I want them to become better, more virtuous people (in ways consistent with our school's stated purposes and projected outcomes for our graduates).*

1	2	3	4	5	6	7	8	9
Not true of me at all								Exactly true of me

3. *I set clearly articulated standards for student academic performance.*

1	2	3	4	5	6	7	8	9

Not true of me at all   *Exactly true of me*

---

4. *I set reasonable, defensible standards for student behavior.*

1	2	3	4	5	6	7	8	9

Not true of me at all   *Exactly true of me*

---

5. *I am continually alert to displays of unkind behavior between and among my students.*

1	2	3	4	5	6	7	8	9

Not true of me at all   *Exactly true of me*

---

6. *In confrontations with students, I conduct myself in ways that leave students' dignity intact regardless of the nature of the issue or infraction.*

1	2	3	4	5	6	7	8	9

Not true of me at all   *Exactly true of me*

---

7. *I demonstrate believably high levels of enthusiasm for teaching/learning and for the content of my studies.*

1	2	3	4	5	6	7	8	9

Not true of me at all   *Exactly true of me*

---

8. *I demonstrate through words and actions a genuine, believable commitment to the school, its purposes, its leadership, and my peers.*

1	2	3	4	5	6	7	8	9

Not true of me at all   *Exactly true of me*

9. *I am glad to arrive at school and to see my students each day.*

1	2	3	4	5	6	7	8	9

Not true of me at all   *Exactly true of me*

10. *I create predictable tests (not to be confused either with "simple" tests or with "easy" tests). My students can rely on the test preparation that I offer them.*

1	2	3	4	5	6	7	8	9

Not true of me at all   *Exactly true of me*

11. *I provide fair, reliable, understandable grade/reward structures for my students. My students are led to understand why they receive the grades they receive—good or bad—and thereby to see how improvement, if they will seek it, might be possible.*

1	2	3	4	5	6	7	8	9

Not true of me at all   *Exactly true of me*

12. *I enforce our rules, including the dress code, justly, fairly, consistently.*

1	2	3	4	5	6	7	8	9

Not true of me at all   *Exactly true of me*

13. *I am able to present myself each day in ways that will be seen by my students as consistent and reliable (i.e., unaffected by outside-of-school problems).*

1	2	3	4	5	6	7	8	9

Not true of me at all   *Exactly true of me*

Part B

The following continuation of CPE II comprises a more comprehensive list of faculty and faculty-culture characteristics designed for use in faculty-culture enhancement systems, career-long faculty professional development systems, faculty evaluation systems, faculty pay-for-performance systems, and faculty hiring/dismissal procedures.

This list has been developed by ISM in conjunction with its personnel-management approach, known since the 1990s as "MFE: Faculty Professional Development and Renewal." While the items following do not tie explicitly to the findings of the ISM Student Experience Study (SES) project, and, thus, not explicitly to the current findings related to student performance, student satisfaction, and student enthusiasm, these items do connect to the seminal six-year 1990s project in which ISM developed the basic foundation on top of which the SES was constructed.

Circle only one number for each item.

14. I pursue career-long professional development as a foremost priority.

1	2	3	4	5	6	7	8	9

Not true of me at all   *Exactly true of me*

15. I am knowledgeable of cutting-edge content and developmental theory.

1	2	3	4	5	6	7	8	9

Not true of me at all   *Exactly true of me*

16. I have mastered at least one pedagogical approach that is supported by reliable, contemporary research outcomes.

1	2	3	4	5	6	7	8	9

Not true of me at all   *Exactly true of me*

17. I am practiced in establishing meaningful emotional/psychological engagement with all my students.

1	2	3	4	5	6	7	8	9

Not true of me at all   *Exactly true of me*

18. I am practiced in finding creative and appropriate ways to be involved with my students outside the classroom.

1	2	3	4	5	6	7	8	9

Not true of me at all   Exactly true of me

19. I am practiced in displaying an overt, conspicuous interest in students' outside-the-class lives—apart from the previous item—without crossing privacy barriers.

1	2	3	4	5	6	7	8	9

Not true of me at all   Exactly true of me

20. I am practiced in applying any subject matter to real-life conditions beyond the classroom, including applications that may be global or universal in their potential.

1	2	3	4	5	6	7	8	9

Not true of me at all   Exactly true of me

21. I am practiced in providing private and public positive reinforcement for individual or group (student) successes.

1	2	3	4	5	6	7	8	9

Not true of me at all   Exactly true of me

22. I am practiced in giving active support for, and establishing active engagement with, colleagues.

1	2	3	4	5	6	7	8	9

Not true of me at all   Exactly true of me

23. I am practiced in making positive contributions to a professional, mission-focused sense of community with all constituent groups.

1	2	3	4	5	6	7	8	9

Not true of me at all   Exactly true of me

24. *I am practiced in establishing proactive communication with, and service to, each student's parents.*

1	2	3	4	5	6	7	8	9

Not true of me at all   Exactly true of me

25. *I am practiced in making an overt commitment to the personal and professional well-being of colleagues, administrators, and (other) nonteaching staff.*

1	2	3	4	5	6	7	8	9

Not true of me at all   Exactly true of me

26. *I am practiced in giving public support for students, colleagues, and employers (administration and Board).*

1	2	3	4	5	6	7	8	9

Not true of me at all   Exactly true of me

27. *I am practiced in communicating in-class experimentation-and-testing outcomes and findings to colleagues, within and beyond the school.*

1	2	3	4	5	6	7	8	9

Not true of me at all   Exactly true of me

28. *I am practiced in routine (yet enthusiastic) participation in outside-the-school academic organizations whose work is supportive of, and pertinent to, my field(s).*

1	2	3	4	5	6	7	8	9

Not true of me at all   Exactly true of me

NOTE: Items 29–35 pertain to schools that are religiously affiliated.

29. *I am practiced in making an overt commitment to the life of my own congregation (church, synagogue, etc.) and its core traditions.*

1	2	3	4	5	6	7	8	9

Not true of me at all   Exactly true of me

30. *I am practiced in serving as a mature role model for a biblically focused lifestyle.*

1	2	3	4	5	6	7	8	9

Not true of me at all   *Exactly true of me*

31. *I am skilled in articulating the personal/ethical implications of a lifelong faith commitment.*

1	2	3	4	5	6	7	8	9

Not true of me at all   *Exactly true of me*

32. *I am practiced in displaying appropriate levels of public tolerance of, and respect for, other religious points of view.*

1	2	3	4	5	6	7	8	9

Not true of me at all   *Exactly true of me*

33. *I am knowledgeable of the developmental history of my school's religious heritage.*

1	2	3	4	5	6	7	8	9

Not true of me at all   *Exactly true of me*

34. *I am practiced in participating in (and when appropriate, leading) the explicitly religious components of the school's student and community programs.*

1	2	3	4	5	6	7	8	9

Not true of me at all   *Exactly true of me*

35. *I am committed to growing professionally and personally within the framework of my religious traditions.*

1	2	3	4	5	6	7	8	9

Not true of me at all   *Exactly true of me*

Most important area(s) to focus on:

SECTION THREE: Objectives

Section Three builds on the previous pages to encourage you to translate your work to this point—school mission statement, personal/ professional mission statement, delineation of professional excellence elements in your professional context—into a very small number of major evaluation/renewal objectives for the next school year. Only two spaces are provided for writing your major objectives because, if they are "major," they deserve **sustained** attention from you throughout the year. To undertake more than two such objectives would provide little more than a recipe for failure; faculty evaluation/renewal, like classroom instruction, is designed for success.

If you and/or your faculty leaders (Head, Division Head, Grade-Level Coordinator, Department Chair, or others who will support you in this process) feel it is, in addition, helpful to utilize a more comprehensive list of objectives this year, simply attach those (presumably generic) items to this page. Please bear in mind, however, that if any of those "extra" objectives qualify as major, then they should substitute for the objectives you develop in these pages—or you invite failure through sheer overload. In other words, if routine objectives (e.g., attend all faculty meetings) are added and easily accommodated, then the major objectives can still be achieved.

The most likely candidate for inclusion in Section Three is the "Professional Excellence" element in your own Section Two, which you marked as your most important focus area.

Examples

"Upgrade my personal system of staying abreast of significant instructional research in middle school social studies."

"Develop stronger approaches to more fully understand the concerns of my students' parents, and develop more reliable ways to address those concerns without compromising my commitment to sound, research-derived instructional methods ... and learn to be less defensive when parents ask questions of me."

ISM recommends that you:

- Limit your objectives to two

- Ensure your objectives are higher order, likely to make a difference to your students and promote your own long-term (strategic) growth

Your Evaluation/Renewal Objectives:

1.

_____

_____

_____

_____

_____

Current self-estimated level of excellence or accomplishment:

1	2	3	4	5	6	7	8	9
Low								High

2.

_____

_____

_____

_____

_____

Current self-estimated level of excellence or accomplishment:

1	2	3	4	5	6	7	8	9
Low								High

SECTION FOUR: Route Descriptions

Use the **Route Description** blank spaces in Section Four to describe the route(s) to your objectives listed in Section Three. Your administrator may ask you to take a particular approach or leave you the choice. With either approach, remember that the outcome is still intended to be the enhancement of student performance, satisfaction, and enthusiasm.

Example

If in Section Three you listed as a major objective, "Upgrade my personal system of staying abreast of significant instructional research in middle-school social studies," you might, on the next page (Section Four), write Route Descriptions such as:

"I will, by August 31, join a middle-school social studies teachers' association and subscribe to its journal."

"I will allocate three hours per month to review a social studies journal's summaries and updates of relevant instructional research."

"I will discuss by August 31, with my Division Head (or other supervisor), an arrangement by which I will, on a quarterly basis, discuss these journal findings in division (or other appropriate) meetings—preferably in settings in which my colleagues will take their turns discussing similar research review processes of their own devising."

… (continue) …

In the previous paragraph's sample Route Description, you have committed yourself to do what you wrote (in this hypothetical example) as a major objective for yourself for the academic year to "upgrade my personal system of staying abreast of … research." You have done so by committing yourself: (a) to join an association that has a journal in which research in your field is reported; (b) to designate three-hour blocks of time each month to review material in the journal; (c) to speak with an appropriate faculty leader about discussing your journal findings with colleagues on a quarterly basis; (d) and more.

Use the **Route Completion Aids** blanks to list the names of colleagues, journals, networks, associations, and other sources of assistance in reaching your major objectives.

You might write in these spaces (Route Completion Aids) the names of several journals and/ or associations that review research on middle school social studies; this might include upper school history journals, adolescent social development journals, political science review journals, learning styles research journals, or any potentially rich, research-derived idea sources. You might, in addition, list an Internet source with potential to place you within a network that regularly discusses research-derived middle school social studies concepts.

With your supervisor, create a calendaring process to schedule the implementation of your ideas and to assist you with the formidable time-management issues implicit in any serious approach to making faculty evaluation/renewal a meaningful experience for you and your colleagues.

For each of the objectives that you have listed in Section Three, write specific action steps you plan to take to attain your objectives. As shown in the examples above, the routes to each objective should have several components.

Route Description, Objective No. 1:

_____

_____

_____

_____

_____

Route Completion Aids, Objective No. 1:

_____

_____

_____

_____

_____

Route Description, Objective No. 2:

_____

_____

_____

_____

_____

Route Completion Aids, Objective No. 2:

_____

_____

_____

_____

_____

SECTION FIVE: *Criteria for Excellence*

Please use the blank spaces in Section Five to specify your criteria for excellence—i.e., your proposed means of knowing the levels of excellence you achieve in the pursuit of your major objectives in the coming year. This may be a novel activity, since conventional approaches to faculty evaluation simply require supervisory personnel to enter your classroom several times a year to observe you in your instructional role. Even when this is well and thoughtfully done, the capacity for such a system to become meaningful in your evaluation/renewal life cycle may not be as large as alternatives.

The system suggested here implies that something different may often be called for. It implies that, while you may indeed be observed in your classroom at times during the school year, the observation(s) will be designed primarily to assist your progression toward your objectives. Consider the middle school social studies example from the previous pages, which is worded as follows: "Upgrade my personal system of staying abreast of significant instructional research in middle-school social studies." Note that this objective is not directly observable. You will surely document the fact that you have "upgraded your personal system," but no one can observe that directly just by visiting your classroom.

Among the implications of this approach is the need for you to be creative in completing Section Five. Please re-examine your objectives (Section Three). What does each imply relative to how you establish a means-of-knowing?

Your means-of-knowing list may include:

- a product (e.g., a log, a diary, a portfolio, a video, a report);

- a result of your efforts (e.g., a new instructional technique, mastery of a new piece of software or computer technology, a new approach to grouping students for particular activities, a new class-control approach, a revised parent education plan);

- an assessment point (e.g., a Division Head's assessment of the product and/or result); and/or

- an assessment process (e.g., a parent survey or a standardized testing event).

Your criteria for excellence should, above all, fit well with your objectives (Section Three), with your Route Descriptions (Section Four), and with the chief underlying assumption in this approach to faculty development and renewal: **Every component should be meaningful to you, both while you do it and after it is completed.**

List a set of "criteria for excellence"—i.e., ways that you will know, through products and results, the levels of excellence you have achieved in pursuit of your objectives.

Criteria for Objective No. 1 (from Section Three)—product, result, assessment point, and/or assessment process:

_____

_____

_____

_____

Objective No. 1: Final self-estimated level of excellence or accomplishment (to be completed at the **conclusion** of the school year and/or the evaluation cycle):

1	2	3	4	5	6	7	8	9

Low   High

Criteria for Objective No. 2 (from Section Three)—product, result, assessment point, and/or assessment process:

_____

_____

_____

_____

Objective No. 2: Final self-estimated level of excellence or accomplishment (to be completed at the **conclusion** of the school year and/or the evaluation cycle):

1	2	3	4	5	6	7	8	9

Low   High